George Meredith

Lord Ormont And His Aminta

A Novel

George Meredith

Lord Ormont And His Aminta
A Novel

ISBN/EAN: 9783337029869

Printed in Europe, USA, Canada, Australia, Japan

Cover: Foto ©Thomas Meinert / pixelio.de

More available books at **www.hansebooks.com**

LORD ORMONT AND HIS AMINTA

A Novel

BY

GEORGE MEREDITH

IN THREE VOLUMES

VOL. I.

LONDON: CHAPMAN AND HALL, Ld.

1894

[All rights reserved]

Gratefully Inscribed

TO

GEORGE BUCKSTON BROWNE,

SURGEON.

CONTENTS OF VOLUME I.

CHAP.		PAGE
I.	LOVE AT A SCHOOL	1
II.	LADY CHARLOTTE	39
III.	THE TUTOR	77
IV.	RECOGNITION	118
V.	IN WHICH THE SHADES OF BROWNY AND MATEY ADVANCE AND RETIRE	140
VI.	IN A MOOD OF LANGUOR	169
VII.	EXHIBITS EFFECTS OF A PRATTLER'S DOSES	200
VIII.	MRS. LAWRENCE FINCHLEY	219

LORD ORMONT AND HIS AMINTA.

CHAPTER I.

LOVE AT A SCHOOL.

A PROCESSION of schoolboys having to meet a procession of schoolgirls on the Sunday's dead march, called a walk, round the park, could hardly go by without dropping to a hum in its chatter, and the shot of incurious half-eyes at the petticoated creatures—all so much of a swarm unless you stare at them like lanterns. The boys cast a glance because it relieved their heaviness; things were lumpish and gloomy that day of the week. The girls, who sped their peep of inquisition before the moment of transit, let it be seen that they had minds occupied with thoughts of their own.

Our gallant fellows forgot the intrusion of the foreign body as soon as it had passed. A sarcastic discharge was jerked by chance at the usher and the governess—at the old game, it seemed; or why did they keep steering the columns to meet? There was no fun in meeting; and it would never be happening every other Sunday, and oftener, by sheer toss-penny accident. They were moved like pieces for the pleasure of these two.

Sometimes the meeting occurred twice during the stupid march-out, when it became so nearly vexatious to boys almost biliously oppressed by the tedium of a day merely allowing them to shove the legs along, ironically naming it animal exercise, that some among them pronounced the sham variation of monotony to be a bothering nuisance if it was going to happen every Sunday, though Sunday required diversions. They hated the absurdity in this meeting and meeting; for they were obliged to anticipate it, as a part of their ignominious weekly performance; and they could not avoid reflecting on it, as a thing done over again: it had them in front and in rear; and it was a kind of broadside mirror, flashing at them the exact opposite of themselves in an identically similar situation, that forced a resemblance.

Touching the old game, Cuper's fold was a healthy school, owing to the good lead of the head boy, Matey Weyburn, a lad with a heart for games to bring renown, and no thought about girls. His emulation, the fellows fancied, was for getting the school into a journal of the Sports. He used to read one sent him by a sporting officer of his name, and talk enviously of public schools, printed whatever they did—a privilege and dignity of which they had unrivalled enjoyment in the past days, when wealth was more jealously exclusive; and he was always prompting for challenges and saving up to pay expenses; and the fellows were to laugh at kicks and learn the art of self-defence—train to rejoice in whipcord muscles. The son of a tradesman, if a boy fell under the imputation, was worthy of honour with him, let the fellow but show grip and toughness. He loathed a skulker, and his face was known for any boy who would own to fatigue or confess himself beaten. "Go to bed," was one of his terrible stings. Matey was good at lessons, too—liked them; liked Latin and Greek; would help a poor stumbler.

Where he did such good work was in sharpening the fellows to excel. He kept them to the grindstone, so that they had no time for rusty brooding; and it was not done by exhortations off a pedestal, like St. Paul at the Athenians. It breathed out of him every day of the week. He carried a light for followers. Whatever he demanded of them, he himself did it easily. He would say to boys "You're going to be men," meaning something better than women. There was a notion that Matey despised girls. Consequently, never much esteemed, they were in disfavour. The old game was mentioned only because of a tradition of an usher and governess leering sick eyes until they slunk away round a corner and married, and set up a school for themselves — an emasculate ending. Comment on it came of a design to show that the whole game had been examined and dismissed as uninteresting and profitless.

One of the boys alluded in Matey's presence to their general view upon the part played by womankind on the human stage, confident of a backing; and he had it, in a way: their noble chief whisked the subject was not worth a discussion; but he turned to a younger chap, who said he detested girls, and asked him how about a sister at home; and the youngster coloured, and Matey took him and spun him round, with a friendly tap on the shoulder.

Odd remarks at intervals caused it to be suspected that he had ideas concerning girls. They were high as his head above the school; and there they were left, with Algebra and Homer, for they were not of a sort to inflame; until the boys noticed how he gave up speaking, and fell to hard looking, on the march past Miss Vincent's young ladies. A well-grown girl (calling herself young lady) made usually the left of the second couple from the front of the line of bonnets, and was by consent good-looking, though she was dark enough to get herself named Browny. In the absence of a fair girl of equal height to set beside her, Browny shone.

She had a nice mouth, ready for a smile at the corners; or so it was before Matey let her see that she was his mark. Now she kept her mouth asleep and her eyes half down, up to the moment of her nearing to pass, when the girl opened on him, as if lifting her eyelids from sleep to the window, a full side-look, like a throb, and no disguise—no slyness or boldness either, not a bit of languishing. You might think her heart came quietly out.

The look was like the fall of light on the hills from the first of morning. It lasted half a minute, and left a ruffle for a good half-hour. Even the younger fellows, without knowing what affected them, were moved by the new picture of a girl, as if it had been a frontispiece of a romantic story some day to be read. She looked compelled to look, but consenting and unashamed; at home in submission; just the look that wins observant boys, shrewd as dogs to read by signs, if they are interested in the persons. They read Browny's meaning: that Matey had only to come and snatch her; he was her master, and she was a brave girl, ready to go all over the world with him; had taken to him as he to her, shot for shot. Her taking to the pick of the school was a capital proof that she was of the right sort. To be sure, she could not much help herself.

Some of the boys regretted her not being fair. But, as they felt, and sought to explain, in the manner of the wag of a tail, with elbows and eyebrows to one another's understanding, fair girls could never have let fly such a look; fair girls are softer, woollier, and when they mean to look serious, overdo it by craping solemn; or they pinafore a jigging eagerness, or hoist propriety on a chubby flaxen grin; or else they dart an eye, or they mince and prim and pout, and are sigh-away and dying-ducky, given to girls' tricks. Browny, after all, was the girl for Matey.

She won a victory right away and out of hand, on behalf of her cloud-and-moon sisters, as against the sunny-meadowy; for slanting intermediates are not espied of boys in anything: conquered by Browny, they went over to her colour, equal to arguing, that Venus at her mightiest must have been dark, or she would not have stood a comparison with the forest Goddess of the Crescent, swanning it through a lake—on the leap for the run of the chase—watching the dart, with her humming bow at breast. The fair are simple sugary things, prone to fat, like bread-sops in milk; but the others are milky nuts, good to bite, Lacedæmonian virgins, hard to beat, putting us on our mettle; and they are for heroes, and they can be brave. So these boys felt, conquered by Browny. A sneaking native taste for the forsaken side, known to renegades, hauled at them if her image waned during the week; and it waned a little, but Sunday restored and stamped it.

By a sudden turn the whole upper-school had fallen to thinking of girls, and the meeting on the Sunday was a prospect. One of the day-boarders had a sister in the seminary of Miss Vincent. He was plied to obtain information concerning Browny's name and her parents. He had it pat to hand in answer. No parents came to see her; an aunt came now and then. Her aunt's name was not wanted. Browny's name was Aminta Farrell.

Farrell might pass; Aminta was debated. This female Christian name had a foreign twang; it gave dissatisfaction. Boy after boy had a try at it, with the same effect: you could not speak the name without a pursing of the mouth and a puckering of the nose, beastly to see, as one little fellow reminded them on a day when Matey was in more than common favour, topping a pitch of rapture, for clean bowling, first ball, middle stump on the kick, the best bat of the other eleven in a match; and, says this youngster, drawling, soon after the cheers and claps had subsided to business, "Aminta."

He made it funny by saying it as if to himself and the ground, in a subdued way, while he swung his leg on a half-circle, like a skater, hands in pockets. He was a sly young rascal, innocently precocious enough, and he meant no disrespect either to Browny or to Matey; but he had to run for it, his delivery of the name being so like what was in the breasts of the senior fellows, as to the inferiority of any Aminta to old Matey, that he set them laughing; and Browny was on the field, to reprove them, left of the tea-booth, with her school-mates, part of her head under a scarlet parasol.

A girl with such a name as Aminta might not be exactly up to the standard of old Matey, still, if he thought her so and she had spirit, the school was bound to subscribe; and that look of hers warranted her for taking her share in the story, like the brigand's wife loading guns for him while he knocks over the foremost carabineer on the mountain-ledge below, who drops on his back with a hellish expression.

Browny was then clearly seen all round, instead of only front-face, as on the Sunday in the park, when fellows could not spy backward after passing. The pleasure they had in seeing her all round involved no fresh stores of observation, for none could tell how she tied her back-hair, which was the question put to them by a cynic of a boy, said to be queasy with excess of sisters. They could tell that she was tall for a girl, or tallish—not a maypole. She drank a cup of tea, and ate a slice of bread-and-butter; no cake.

She appeared undisturbed when Matey, wearing his holiday white ducks, and all aglow, entered the booth. She was not expected to faint, only she stood for the foreign Aminta more than for their familiar Browny in his presence. Not a sign of the look which had fired the school did she throw at him. Change the colour and you might compare her to a bolster fixed on end, with a chin and no eyes. Matey talked to Miss Vincent up to the instant of his running to bat. She would have liked to guess how he knew she had a brother on the medical staff of one of the regiments in India: she asked him twice, and his cheeks were redder than cricket in the sun. He said he read all the reports from India, and asked her whether she did not admire Lord Ormont, our general of cavalry, whose charge at the head of fifteen hundred horse in the last great battle shattered the enemy's right wing, and gave us the victory—rolled him up and stretched him out like a carpet for dusting. Miss Vincent exclaimed that it was really strange, now, he should speak of Lord Ormont, for she had been speaking of him herself in the morning to one of her young ladies, whose mind was bent on his heroical deeds. Matey turned his face to the group of young ladies, quite pleased that one of them loved his hero; and he met a smile here and there—not from Miss Aminta Farrell. She was a complete disappointment to the boys that day. "Aminta" was mouthed at any allusion to her.

So, she not being a match for Matey, they let her drop. The flush that had swept across the school withered to a dry recollection, except when on one of their Sunday afternoons she fanned the desert. Lord Ormont became the subject of inquiry

and conversation; and for his own sake—
not altogether to gratify Matey. The
Saturday autumn evening's walk home,
after the race out to tea at a distant village,
too late in the year for cricket, too early for
regular football, suited Matey, going at long
strides, for the story of his hero's adventures; and it was nicer than talk about
girls, and puzzling. Here lay a clear field;
for he had the right to speak of a cavalry
officer: his father died of wounds in the
service, and Matey naturally intended to
join the Dragoons, if he could get enough
money to pay for mess, he said, laughing.
Lord Ormont was his pattern of a warrior.
We had in him a lord who cast off luxury
to live like a Spartan when under arms,
with a passion to serve his country and
sustain the glory of our military annals.
He revived respect for the noble class in
the hearts of Englishmen. He was as good
an authority on horseflesh as any English-

man alive; the best for the management of cavalry: there never was a better cavalry leader. The boys had come to know that Browny admired Lord Ormont, so they saw a double reason why Matey should; and walking home at his grand swing in the October dusk, their school hero drew their national hero closer to them.

Every fellow present was dead against the usher, Mr. Shalders, when he took advantage of a pause to strike in with his "Murat!"

He harped on Murat whenever he had a chance. Now he did it for the purpose of casting eclipse upon Major-General Lord Ormont, the son and grandson of English earls; for he was an earl by his title, and Murat was the son of an innkeeper. Shalders had to admit that Murat might have served in the stables as a boy. Honour to Murat, of course, for climbing the peaks! Shalders, too, might interest himself in military affairs and Murat; he did no harm, and he could be amusing. It rather added to his amount of dignity. It was rather absurd, at the same time, for an English usher to be spouting and glowing about a French General, who had been a stable-boy and became a king, with his Murat this, Murat that, and hurrah Murat in red and white and green uniform, tunic, and breeches, and a chimney-afire of feathers; and how the giant he was charged at the head of ten thousand horse, all going like a cataract under a rainbow over the rocks, right into the middle of the enemy and through; and he a spark ahead, and the enemy streaming on all sides flat away, as you see puffed smoke and flame of a bonfire. That was fun to set boys jigging. No wonder how in Russia the Cossacks feared him, and scampered from the shadow of his plumes—were clouds flying off his breath! That was a fine warm picture for the boys on late autumn or early winter evenings, Shalders warming his back at the grate, describing bivouacs in the snow. They liked well enough to hear him when he was not opposing Matey and Lord Ormont. He perked on his toes, and fetched his hand from behind him to flourish it when his Murat came out. The speaking of the name clapped him on horseback—the only horseback he ever knew. He was as fond of giving out the name Murat as you see in old engravings of tobacco-shops men enjoying the emission of their whiff of smoke.

Matey was not inclined to class Lord Ormont alongside Murat, a first-rate horseman and an eagle-eye, as Shalders rightly said; and Matey agreed that forty thousand cavalry under your orders is a toss above fifteen hundred; but the claim for a Frenchman of a superlative merit to swallow and make nothing of the mention of our best cavalry generals irritated him to call Murat a mountebank.

Shalders retorted, that Lord Ormont was a reprobate.

Matey hoped he would some day write us an essay on the morals of illustrious generals of cavalry; and Shalders told him he did not advance his case by talking nonsense.

Each then repeated to the boys a famous exploit of his hero. Their verdict was favourable to Lord Ormont. Our English General learnt riding before he was ten years old, on the Pampas, where you ride all day, and cook your steak for your dinner between your seat and your saddle. He rode with his father and his uncle, Muncastle, the famous traveller, into Paraguay. He saw fighting before he was twelve. Before he was twenty he was learning outpost duty in the Austrian frontier cavalry. He served in the Peninsula, served in

Canada, served in India, volunteered for any chance of distinction. No need to say much of his mastering the picked Indian swordsmen in single combat: he knew their trick, and was quick to save his reins when they made a dash threatening the head-stroke—about the same as disabling sails in old naval engagements.

That was the part for the officer; we are speaking of the General. For that matter, he had as keen an eye for the field and the moment for his arm to strike as any Murat. One would have liked to see Murat matched against the sabre of a wily Rajpoot! As to campaigns and strategy, Lord Ormont's head was a map. What of Murat and Lord Ormont horse to horse and sword to sword? Come, imagine that, if you are for comparisons. And if Lord Ormont never headed a lot of thousands, it does not prove he was unable. Lord Ormont was as big as Murat. More, he was a Christian to his horses.

How about Murat in that respect? Lord Ormont cared for his men: did Murat so particularly much? And he was as cunning fronting odds, and a thunderbolt at the charge. Why speak of him in the past? He is an English lord, a lord by birth, and he is alive; things may be expected of him to-morrow or next day.

Shalders here cut Matey short by meanly objecting to that.

"Men are mortal," he said, with a lot of pretended stuff, deploring our human condition in the elegy strain; and he fell to reckoning the English hero's age—as that he, Lord Ormont, had been a name in the world for the last twenty-five years or more. The noble lord could be no chicken. We are justified in calculating, by the course of nature, that his term of activity is approaching, or has approached, or, in fact, has drawn to its close.

"If your estimate, sir, approaches to

correctness," rejoined Matey—tellingly, his comrades thought.

"Sixty, as you may learn some day, is a serious age, Matthew Weyburn."

Matey said he should be happy to reach it with half the honours Lord Ormont had won.

"Excepting the duels," Shalders had the impudence to say.

"If the cause is a good one!" cried Matey.

"The cause, or Lord Ormont has been maligned, was reprehensible in the extremest degree." Shalders cockhorsed on his heels to his toes and back with a bang.

"What was the cause, if you please, sir?" a boy, probably naughty, inquired; and, as Shalders did not vouchsafe a reply, the bigger boys knew.

They revelled in the devilish halo of skirts on the whirl encircling Lord Ormont's laurelled head.

That was a spark in their blood struck from a dislike of the tone assumed by Mr. Shalders to sustain his argument; with his "men are mortal," and talk of a true living champion as "no chicken," and the wordy drawl over "justification for calculating the approach of a close to a term of activity"—in the case of a proved hero!

Guardians of boys should make sure that the boys are on their side before they raise the standard of virtue. Nor ought they to summon morality for support of a polemic. Matey Weyburn's object of worship rode superior to a morality puffing its phrasy trumpet. And, somehow, the sacrifice of an enormous number of women to Lord Ormont's glory seemed natural; the very thing that should be, in the case of a first-rate military hero and commander —Scipio notwithstanding. It brightens his flame, and it is agreeable to them. That is how they come to distinction : they have no other chance; they are only women; they are mad to be singed, and they rush pell-mell, all for the honour of the candle.

Shortly after this discussion Matey was heard informing some of the bigger fellows he could tell them positively that Lord Ormont's age was under fifty-four—the prime of manhood, and a jolly long way off death! The greater credit to him, therefore, if he had been a name in the world for anything like the period Shalders insinuated, "to get himself out of a sad quandary." Matey sounded the queer word so as to fix it sticking to the usher, calling him Mr. Peter Bell Shalders, at which the boys roared, and there was a question or two about names, which belonged to verses, for people caring to read poems.

To the joy of the school he displayed a greater knowledge of Murat than Shalders had : named the different places in Europe where Lord Ormont and Murat were both springing to the saddle at the same time— one a Marshal, the other a lieutenant; one a king, to be off his throne any day, the other a born English nobleman, seated firm as fate. And he accused Murat of carelessness of his horses, ingratitude to his benefactor, circussy style. Shalders went so far as to defend Murat for attending to the affairs of his kingdom, instead of galloping over hedges and ditches to swell Napoleon's ranks in distress. Matey listened to him there; he became grave; he nodded like a man saying, "I suppose we must examine it in earnest." The school was damped to hear him calling it a nice question. Still, he said he thought he should have gone; and that settled it.

The boys inclined to speak contemptuously of Shalders. Matey would not let them; he contrasted Shalders with the other ushers, who had no enthusiasms. He said enthusiasms were salt to a man; and he liked Shalders for spelling at his battles and thinking he understood them, and admiring Murat, and reading Virgil and parts of Lucan for his recreation. He said he liked the French because they could be splendidly enthusiastic. He almost lost his English flavour when he spoke in downright approval of a small French fellow, coming from Orthez, near the Pyrenees, for senselessly dashing and kicking at a couple of English who jeered to hear Orthez named— a place trampled under Wellington's heels, on his march across conquered France. The foreign little cockerel was a clever lad, learning English fast, and anxious to show he had got hold of the English trick of not knowing when he was beaten. His French vanity insisted on his engaging the two, though one of them stood aside, and the other let him drive his nose all the compass round at a poker fist. What was worse,

Matey examined these two, in the interests of fair play, as if he doubted.

Little Émile Grenat set matters right with his boast to vindicate his country against double the number, and Matey praised him, though he knew Émile had been floored without effort by the extension of a single fist. He would not hear the French abused; he said they were chivalrous, they were fine fellows, topping the world in some things; his father had fought them and learnt to respect them. Perhaps his father had learnt to respect Jews, for there was a boy named Abner, he protected, who smelt Jewish; he said they ran us Gentiles hard, and carried big guns.

Only a reputation like Matey's could have kept his leadership from a challenge. Joseph Masner, fomerly a rival, went about hinting and shrugging; all to no purpose, you find boys born to be chiefs. On the day of the snow-fight Matey won the toss, and chose J. Masner first pick; and Masner, aged seventeen and some months, big as a navvy, lumbered across to him and took his directions, proud to stand in the front centre, at the head of the attack, and bear the brunt—just what he was fit for. Matey gave no offence by choosing, half-way down the list, his little French friend, whom he stationed beside himself, rather off his battle-front, as at point at cricket, not quite so far removed. Two boys at his heels piled ammunition. The sides met midway of a marshy ground, where a couple of flat and shelving banks, formed for a broad new road, good for ten abreast (counting a step of the slopes), ran transverse; and the order of the game was to clear the bank and drive the enemy on to the frozen ditch-water. Miss Vincent heard in the morning from the sister of little Collett of the great engagement coming off; she was moved by curiosity, and so the young ladies of her establishment beheld the young gentlemen of Mr. Cuper's in furious division, and Matey's sure aim and hard fling, equal to a slinger's, relieving J. Masner of a foremost assailant with a spanker on the nob. They may have fancied him clever for selecting a position rather comfortable, as things went, until they had sight of him with his little French ally and two others, ammunition boys to rear, descending one bank and scaling another right into the flank of the enemy, when his old tower of a Masner was being heavily pressed by numbers. Then came a fight hand to hand, but the enemy stood in a clamp; not to split like a nut between crackers, they gave way and rolled, backing in lumps from bank to ditch.

The battle was over before the young ladies knew. They wondered to see Matey shuffling on his coat and hopping along at easy bounds to pay his respects to Miss Vincent, near whom was Browny; and this time he and Browny talked together. He then introduced little Émile to her. She spoke of Napoleon at Brienne, and complimented Matey. He said he was cavalry, not artillery, that day. They talked to hear one another's voices. By constantly appealing to Miss Vincent he made their conversation together seem as under her conduct; and she took a slide on some French phrases with little Émile. Her young ladies looked shrinking and envious to see the fellows wet to the skin, laughing, wrestling, linking arms; and some, who were clown-faced with a wipe of scarlet, getting friends to rub their cheeks with snow, all of them happy as larks in air, a big tea steaming for them at the school. Those girls had a leap and a fall of the heart, glad to hug themselves in their dry clothes, and not so warm as the dripping boys were, nor so madly fond of their dress-circle seats to look on at a play they were not allowed even to desire to share. They looked on at blows given and taken in good temper, hardship sharpening jollity. The thought of the difference between themselves and the boys must have been something like the tight band—call it corset—over the chest, trying to lift and stretch for draughts of air. But Browny's feeling naturally was, that all this advantage for the boys came of Matey Weyburn's lead.

Miss Vincent with her young ladies walked off in couples, orderly chicks, the usual Sunday march of their every day. The school was coolish to them; one of the fellows hummed bars of some hymn tune, rather faster than church; and next day there was a murmur of letters passing between Matey and Browny regularly, little Collett for postman. Anybody might have guessed it, but the report spread a feeling that girls are not the entirely artificial beings or flat targets we suppose. The school began to brood, like air deadening on oven-heat. Winter is hen-mother to the idea of love in schools, if the idea has fairly entered. Various girls of different colours were selected by boys for animated correspondence, that never existed and was vigorously prosecuted, with efforts to repress contempt of them in courtship for their affections. They found their part of it by no means difficult when they imagined the lines without the words, or, better still, the letter without the lines. A holy satisfaction belonged to the sealed thing; the breaking of the seal and inspection of the contents imposed perplexity on that sentiment. They thought of certain possible sentences Matey and Browny would exchange; but the plain, conceivable, almost visible, outside of the letter had a stronger spell for them than the visionary inside. This fancied contemplation of the love-letter was reversed in them at once by the startling news of Miss Vincent's discovery and seizure of the sealed thing, and her examination of the burden it contained. Then their thirst was for drama—to see, to drink every wonderful syllable those lovers had written.

Miss Vincent's hand was upon one of Matey's letters. She had come across the sister of little Collett, Selina her name was, carrying it. She saw nothing of the others. Aminta was not the girl to let her. Nor did Mr. Cuper dare demand from Matey a sight or restitution of the young lady's half of the correspondence. He preached heavily at Matey; deplored that the boy he most trusted, etc.—the school could have repeated it without hearing. We know the master's lecture in tones—it sings up to sing down, and touches nobody. As soon as he dropped to natural talk, and spoke of his responsibility and Miss Vincent's, Matey gave the word of a man of honour that he would not seek to communicate further with Miss Farrell at the school.

Now there was a regular thunder-hush among the boys on the rare occasions when they met the girls. All that Matey and Browny were forbidden to write they *looked* —much like what it had been before the discovery; and they dragged the boys back from promised instant events. It was, nevertheless, a heaving picture, like the sea in the background of a marine piece at the theatre, which rouses anticipations of storm, and shows readiness. Browny's full eyebrow sat on her dark eye like a cloud of winter noons over the vanishing sun. Matey was the prisoner gazing at light of a barred window and measuring the strength of the bars. She looked unhappy, but looked unbeaten more. Her look at him fed the school on thoughts of what love really is, when it is not fished out of books and poetry. For though she was pale, starved and pale, they could see she was never the one to be sighing; and as for him, he looked ground down all to edge. However much they puzzled over things, she made them feel they were sure, as to her, that she drove straight and meant blood, the life or death of it: all her own, if need be, and confidence in the captain she had chosen. She could have been imagined saying, There's a storm, but I am ready to embark with you this minute.

That sign of courage in real danger ennobled her among girls. The name Browny was put aside for a respectful Aminta. Big and bright events to come out in the world were hinted, from the love of such a couple. The boys were not ashamed to speak the very word love. How he does love that girl! Well, and how she loves him! She did, but the boys had to be seeing her look at Matey if they were to put the girl on some balanced equality with a fellow she was compelled to love. It seemed to them that he gave, and that she was a creature carried to him, like driftwood along the current of the flood, given, in spite of herself. When they saw those eyes of hers they were impressed with an idea of her as a voluntary giver too; pretty well the half to the bargain; and it confused their notion of feminine inferiority. They resolved to think her an exceptional girl, which, in truth, they could easily do, for none but an exceptional girl could win Matey to love her.

Since nothing appeared likely to happen at the school, they speculated upon what would occur out in the world, and were assisted to conjecture by a rumour, telling of Aminta Farrell's aunt as a resident at Dover. Those were days when the benevolently international M. de Porquet had begun to act as interpreter to English schools in the portico of the French language; and under his guidance it was asked, in contempt of the answer, *Combien de postes d'ici à Douvres?* But, accepting the rumour as a piece of information, the answer became important. *Ici* was twenty miles to the north-west of London. How long would it take Matey to reach Douvres? Or at which of the *combien* did he intend to waylay and away with Aminta? The boys went about pounding at the interrogative French phrase in due sincerity, behind the burlesque of traveller bothering coachman. Matey's designs could be guessed only by a knowledge of his character: that he was not the fellow to give up the girl he had taken to; and impediments might multiply; but he would bear them down. Three days before the break-up of the school another rumour came tearing through it: Aminta's aunt had withdrawn her from Miss Vincent's. And now rose the question, two-dozen-mouthed, Did Matey know her address at Douvres? His face grew stringy and his voice harder, and his eyes ready to burst from a smother of fire. All the same he did his work: he was the good old fellow at games, considerate in school affairs, kind to the youngsters; he was heard to laugh. He liked best the company of his little French friend from Orthez, over whose shoulder his hand was laid sometimes as they strolled and chatted in two languages. He really went a long way to make French fellows popular, and the boys were sorry that little Émile was off to finish his foreign education in Germany. His English was pretty good, thanks to Matey. He went away, promising to remember Old England, saying he was French first, and a Briton next. He had lots of pluck; which accounted for Matey's choice of him as a friend among the juniors.

CHAPTER II.

LADY CHARLOTTE.

LOVE-PASSAGES at a school must produce a ringing crisis if they are to leave the rosy impression which spans the gap of holidays. Neither Matey nor Browny returned to their yoke, and Cuper's boys recollected the couple chiefly on Sundays. They remembered several of Matey's doings and sayings: his running and high leaping, his bowling, a maxim or two of his, and the tight strong fellow he was; also that the damsel's colour distinctly counted for dark. She became nearly black in their minds. Well, and Englishmen have been known to marry Indian princesses: some have a liking for negresses. There are Nubians rather pretty in pictures, if you can stand thick lips. Her colour does not matter, provided the girl is of the right sort. The exchange of letters between the lovers was mentioned. The discovery by Miss Vincent of their cool habit of corresponding passed for an incident; and there it remained, stiff as a post, not being heated by a story to run. So the foregone excitement lost warmth, and went out like a winter sun at noon or a match lighted before the candle is handy.

Lord Ormont continued to be a subject of discussion from time to time, for he was a name in the newspapers; and Mr. Shalders had been worked by Matey Weyburn into a state of raw antagonism at the mention of the gallant General; he could not avoid sitting in judgment on him.

According to Mr. Shalders, the opinion of all thoughtful people in England was with John Company and the better part of the Press to condemn Lord Ormont in his quarrel with the Commissioner of one of the Indian provinces, who had the support of the Governor of his Presidency and of the Viceroy; the latter not unreservedly, yet ostensibly inclined to condemn a too prompt military hand. The Gordian knot of a difficulty cut is agreeable in the contemplation of an official chief hesitating to use the sword and benefiting by having it done for him. Lord Ormont certainly cut the knot.

Mr. Shalders was cornered by the boys, coming at him one after another without a stop, vowing it was the exercise of a military judgment upon a military question at a period of urgency, which had brought about the quarrel with the Commissioner and the reproof of the Governor. He betrayed the man completely cornered by generalizing. He said—

"We are a civilian people; we pride ourselves on having civilian methods."

"How can that be if we have won India with guns and swords?"

"But that splendid jewel for England's tiara won," said he (and he might as well have said crown), "we are bound to sheathe the sword and govern by the Book of the Law."

"But if they won't have the Book of the Law!"

"They know the power behind it."

"Not if we knock nothing harder than the Book of the Law upon their skulls."

"Happily for the country, England's councils are not directed by boys!"

"Ah, but we're speaking of India, Mr. Shalders."

"You are presuming to speak of an act of insubordination committed by a military officer under civilian command."

"What if we find an influential Indian prince engaged in conspiracy?"

"We look for proof."

"Suppose we have good proof?"

"We summon him to exonerate himself."

"No, we mount and ride straight away into his territory, spot the treason, deport him, and rule in his place!"

It was all very well for Mr. Shalders to say he talked to boys; he was cornered again, as his shrug confessed.

The boys asked among themselves whether he would have taken the same view if his Murat had done it!

These illogical boys fought for Matey Weyburn in their defence of Lord Ormont. Somewhere, they were sure, old Matey was hammering to the same end—they could hear him. Thought of him inspired them to unwonted argumentative energy, that they might support his cause, and scatter the gloomy prediction of the school, as going to the dogs now Matey had left.

The subject provoked everywhere in Great

Britain a division similar to that between master and boys at Cuper's establishment: one party for our modern English magisterial methods with Indians, the other for the decisive Oriental at the early time, to suit their native tastes; and the Book of the Law is to be conciliatingly addressed to their sentiments by a benign civilizing Power, or the sword is out smartly at the hint of a warning to protect the sword's conquests. Under one aspect we appear potteringly European; under another, drunk of the East.

Lord Ormont's ride at the head of two hundred horsemen across a stretch of country including hill and forest, to fall like a bolt from the blue on the suspected Prince in the midst of his gathering warriors, was a handsome piece of daring, and the high-handed treatment of the Prince was held by his advocates to be justified by the provocation and the result. He scattered an unprepared body of many hundreds, who might have enveloped him, and who would presumptively have stood their ground, had they not taken his handful to be the advance of regiments. These are the deeds that win empires! the argument in his favour ran. Are they of a character to maintain empires? the counter-question was urged. Men of a deliberative aspect were not wanting in approval of the sharp and summary of the sword in air when we have to deal with Indians. They chose to regard it as a matter of the dealing with Indians, and put aside the question of the contempt of civil authority.

Counting the cries, Lord Ormont won his case. Festival aldermen, smoking clubmen, buckskin squires, obsequious yet privately excitable tradesmen, sedentary coachmen and cabmen, of Viking descent, were set to think like boys about him: and the boys, the women, and the poets formed a tipsy chorus. Journalists, on the whole, were fairly halved, as regarded numbers. In relation to weight, they were with the burgess and the presbyter; they preponderated heavily in the direction of England's burgess view of all cases disputed between civilian and soldier. But that was when the peril was over.

Admirers of Lord Ormont enjoyed a perusal of a letter addressed by him to the burgess's journal; and so did his detractors. The printing of it was an act of editorial ruthlessness. The noble soldier had no mould in his intellectual or educational foundry for the casting of sentences; and the editor's leading type to the letter, without further notice of the writer—who was given a prominent place or scaffolding for the execution of himself publicly, if it pleased him to do that thing—tickled the critical mind. Lord Ormont wrote intemperately.

His Titanic hurling of blocks against critics did no harm to an enemy skilled in the use of trimmer weapons, notably the fine one of letting big missiles rebound. He wrote from India, with Indian heat— " curry and capsicums," it was remarked. He dared to claim the countenance of the Commander-in-chief of the Army of India for an act disapproved by the India House. Other letters might be on their way, curryer than the preceding, his friends feared; and might also be malevolently printed, similarly commissioning the reverberation of them to belabour his name before the public. Admirers were still prepared to admire; but aldermen not at the feast, squirearchs not in the saddle or at the bottle, some few of the juvenile and female fervent, were becoming susceptible to a frosty critical tone in the public pronunciation of Lord Ormont's name since the printing of his letter and the letters it called forth. None of them doubted that his case was good. The doubt concerned the effect on it of his manner of pleading it. And if he damaged his case, he compromised his admirers. Why, the case of a man who has cleverly won a bold stroke for his country must be good, as long as he holds his tongue. A grateful country will right him in the end : he has only to wait, and not so very long. "This I did : now examine it." Nothing more needed to be said by him, if that.

True, he has a temper. It is owned that he is a hero. We take him with his qualities, impetuosity being one, and not unsuited to his arm of the service, as he has shown. If his temper is high, it is an element of a character proved heroical. So has the sun his blotches, and we believe that they go to nourish the luminary, rather than that they are a disease of the photosphere.

Lord Ormont's apologists had to contend with anecdotes and dicta now pouring in from offended Britons, for illustration of an impetuosity fit to make another Charles XII. of Sweden—a gratuitous Coriolanus haughtiness as well, new among a people accustomed socially to bow the head to their nobles, and not, of late, expecting a kick for their pains. Newspapers wrote of him that, "a martinet to subordinates, he was known for the most unruly of lieutenants." They alluded to current sayings, as that he "habitually took counsel of his horse on the field when a movement was entrusted to his discretion." Numerous were the journalistic sentences running under an air of eulogy of the lordly warrior purposely to be tripped, and producing their damnable effect, despite the obvious artifice. The writer of the letter from Bombay, signed Ormont, was a born subject for the antithetical craftsmen's tricky springes.

He was, additionally, of infamous repute for morals in burgess estimation, from his having a keen appreciation of female beauty and a prickly sense of masculine honour. The stir to his name roused pestilential domestic stories. In those days the aristocrat still claimed licence, and eminent soldier-nobles, comporting themselves as imitative servants of their god Mars, on the fields of love and war, stood necessarily prepared to vindicate their conduct on the field of the measured paces, without deeming themselves bounden to defend the course they took. Our burgess, who bowed head to his aristocrat, and hired the soldier to fight for him, could not see that such misbehaviour necessarily ensued. Lord Ormont had fought duels at home and abroad. His readiness to fight again, and against odds, and with a totally unused weapon, was exhibited by his attack on the Press in the columns of the Press. It wore the comical face to the friends deploring it, which belongs to things we do that are so very like us. They agreed with his devoted sister, Lady Charlotte Eglett, as to the prudence of keeping him out of England for a time, if possible.

At the first perusal of the letter, Lady Charlotte quitted her place in Leicestershire, husband, horses, guests, the hunt, to scour across a vacant London and pick up acquaintances under stress to be spots there in the hunting season, with them to gossip for counsel on the subject of "Ormont's hand-grenade," and how to stop and extinguish a second. She was a person given to plain speech. "Stinkpot" she called it, when acknowledging foul elements in the composition and the harm it did to the unskilful balist. Her view of the burgess English imaged a mighty monster behind bars, to whom we offer anything but our hand. As soon as he gets hold of that he has you; he won't let it loose with flesh on the bones. We must offend him—

we can't be man or woman without offending his tastes and his worships; but while we keep from contact (*i. e.* intercommunication) he may growl, he is harmless. Witness the many occasions when her brother offended worse, and had been unworried, only growled at, and distantly, not in a way to rouse concern; and at the next review, or procession into the City, or public display of any sort, Ormont had but to show himself, he was the popular favourite immediately. He had not committed the folly of writing a letter to a newspaper then.

Lady Charlotte paid an early visit to the office of the great London solicitor, Arthur Abner, who wielded the Law as an instrument of protection for countless illustrious people afflicted by what they stir or attract in a wealthy metropolis. She went simply to gossip of her brother's affairs with a refreshing man of the world, not given to circumlocutions, and not afraid of her: she had no deeper object; but fancying she heard the clerk, on his jump from the stool, inform her that Mr. Abner was out, " Out?" she cried, and rattled the room, thumping, under knitted brows. " Out of town?" For a man of business taking holidays, when a lady craves for gossip, disappointed her faith in him as cruelly as the shut-up, empty inn the broken hunter knocking at a hollow door miles off home.

Mr. Abner, hatted and gloved and smiling, came forth. " ' Going out,' the man meant, Lady Charlotte. At your service for five minutes."

She complimented his acuteness in the remark, " You see I've only come to chat," and entered his room.

He led her to her theme: " The excitement is pretty well over."

" My brother's my chief care—always was. I'm afraid he'll be pitchforking at it again, and we shall have another blast.

That letter ought never to have been printed. That editor deserves the horsewhip for letting it appear. If he prints a second one I shall treat him as a personal enemy."

"Better make a friend of him."

"How?"

"Meet him at my table."

She jumped an illumined half-about on her chair. "So I will, then. What are the creature's tastes?"

"Hunting will do."

"Hunts, does he?" The editor rose in her mind from the state of neuter to something of a man. "I recollect an article in that paper on the Ormont duel. I hate duelling, but I side with my brother. I had to laugh, though. Luckily, there's no woman on hand at present, as far as I know. Ormont's not likely to be hooked by garrison women or blacks. Those coloured women—some of ours too—send the nose to the clouds; not a bad sign for health. And there are men like that old Cardinal Guicciardini tells of . . . hum! Ormont's not one of them. I hope he'll stay in India till this blows over, or I shall be hearing of provocations."

"You have seen the Duke?"

She nodded. Her reserve was a summary of the interview. "Kind, as he always is," she said. "Ormont has no chance of employment unless there's a European war. They can't overlook him in case of war. He'll have to pray for that."

"Let us hope we shan't get it."

"My wish; but I have to think of my brother. If he's in England with no employment, he's in a mess with women and men both. He kicks if he's laid aside to rust. He has a big heart. That's what I said : all he wants is to serve his country. If you won't have war, give him Gibraltar or Malta, or command of one of our military districts. The South-eastern 'll be vacant soon. He'd like to be Constable of the Castle, and have an eye on France."

"I think he's fond of the French?"

"Loves the French. Expects to have to fight them all the same. He loves his country best. Here's the man everybody's abusing!"

"I demur, my lady. I was dining the other day with a client of mine, and a youngster was present who spoke of Lord Ormont in a way I should like you to have heard. He seemed to know the whole of Lord Ormont's career, from the time of the ride to Paraguay up to the capture of the plotting Rajah. He carried the table."

"Good boy! We must turn to the boys for justice, then. Name your day for this man, this editor."

"I will see him. You shall have the day to-night."

Lady Charlotte and the editor met. She

was racy, he anecdotal. Stag, fox, and hare ran before them, over fields and through drawing-rooms: the scent was rich. They found that they could talk to one another as they thought; that he was not the Isle-bound burgess, nor she the postured English great lady; and they exchanged salt, without which your current scandal is of exhausted savour. They enjoyed the peculiar novel relish of it, coming from a social pressman and a dame of high society. The different hemispheres became known as one sphere to these birds of broad wing convening in the upper blue above a quartered carcase earth.

A week later a letter, the envelope of a bulky letter in Lord Ormont's handwriting, reached Lady Charlotte. There was a line from the editor:

"*Would it please your ladyship to have this printed?*"

She read the letter, and replied:

"*Come to me for six days; you shall have the best mount in the county.*"

An editor devoid of malice might probably have forborne to print a letter that appealed to Lady Charlotte, or touched her sensations, as if a glimpse of the moon, on the homeward ride in winter on a nodding horse, had suddenly bared to view a precipitous quarry within two steps. There is no knowing: few men can forbear to tell a spicy story of their friends; and an editor, to whom an exhibition of the immensely preposterous on the part of one writing arrogantly must be provocative, would feel the interests of his journal, not to speak of the claims of readers, pluck at him when he meditated the consignment of such a precious composition to extinction. Lady Charlotte withheld a sight of the letter from Mr. Eglett. She laid it in her desk, understanding well that it was a laugh lost to the world. Poets could reasonably feign it to shake the desk inclosing it. She had a strong sense of humour; her mind reverted to the desk in a way to make her lips shut grimly. She sided with her brother.

Only pen in hand did he lay himself open to the enemy. In his personal intercourse he was the last of men to be taken at a disadvantage. Lady Charlotte was brought round to the distasteful idea of some help coming from a legitimate adjunct at his elbow: a restraining woman—wife, it had to be said. And to name the word wife for Thomas Rowsley, Earl of Ormont, put up the porcupine quills she bristled with at the survey of a sex thirsting, and likely to continue thirsting, for such honour. What woman had she known fit to bear the name? She had assumed the judicial seat upon the pretensions of several, and dismissed them to their limbo, after testifying against them. Who is to know the fit one in these mines of deception? Women of the class offering wives decline to be taken on trial; they are boxes of puzzles—often dire surprises. Her brother knew them well enough to shy at the box. Her brother Rowsley had a funny pride, like a boy at a game, at the never having been caught by one among the many he made captive. She let him have it all to himself.

He boasted it to a sister sharing the pride—exultant in the cry of the hawk, scornful of ambitious poultry, a passed finger-post to the plucked, and really regretful that no woman had been created fit for him. When she was not siding with her brother, women, however contemptible for their weakness, appeared to her as better than barn-door fowl, or vermin in their multitudes gnawing to get at the

cheese-trap. She could be humane, even
sisterly, with women whose conduct or
prattle did not outrage plain sense, just
as the stickler for the privileges of her
class was large-heartedly charitable to the
classes flowing in oily orderliness round
about below it—if they did so flow. Unable
to read woman's character, except upon
the broadest lines, as it were the spider's
main threads of its web, she read men
minutely, from the fact that they were
neither mysteries nor terrors to her, but
creatures of importunate appetites, humorous
objects; very manageable, if we leave the
road to their muscles, dress their wounds,
smoothe their creases, plume their vanity;
and she had an unerring eye for the man
to be used when a blow was needed,
methods for setting him in action likewise.
She knew how much stronger than ordinary
men the woman who can put them in
motion. They can be set to serve as pieces

of cannon, under compliments on their superior powers, which were not all undervalued by her on their own merits, for she worshipped strength. But she said, with a certain amount of truth, that the women unaware of the advantage Society gave them (as to mastering men) were fools.

Tender, is not a word coming near to Lady Charlotte. Thoughtful on behalf of the poor foolish victims of men she was. She had saved some, avenged others. It should be stated that her notion of saving was the saving of them from the public: she had thrown up a screen. The saving of them from themselves was another matter—hopeless, to her thinking. How preach at a creature on the bend of passion's rapids! One might as well read a chapter from the Bible to delirious patients. When once a woman is taken from the love-passion, we must treat her as bitten; hide her antics from the public: that is the principal business. If she recovers, she resumes her place, and horrid old Nature, who drove her to the frenzy, is unlikely to bother or, at least, overthrow her again, unless she is one of the detestable wantons, past compassion or consideration. In the case reviewed, the woman has gone through fire, and is none the worse for her experiences: worth ten times what she was, to an honest man, if men could be got to see it. Some do. Of those men who do not, Lady Charlotte spoke with the old family-nurse humour, which is familiar with the tricks and frailties of the infants; and it is a knife to probe the male, while seemingly it does the part of the napkin—pities and pats. They expect a return of much for the little that is next to nothing. They are full of expectations: and of what else? They are hard bargainers.

She thought this of men; and she liked men by choice. She had old nurse's preference for the lustier male child. The others are puling things, easier to rear, because they bend better; and less esteemed, though they give less trouble, rouse less care. But when it came to the duel between the man and the woman, her sense of justice was moved to join her with the party of her unfairly handled sisters—a strong party, if it were not so cowardly, she had to think.

Mr. Eglett, her husband, accepted her— accepted the position into which he naturally fell beside her, and the ideas she imposed on him; for she never went counter to his principles. These were the fixed principles of a very wealthy man, who abhorred debt, and was punctilious in veracity, scrupulous in cleanliness of mind and body, devoted to the honour of his country, the interests of his class. She respected the high landmark possessing such principles, and she was therefore enabled to lead without the wish to rule. As it had been between them at the beginning, so it was now, when they were grandparents running on three lines of progeny from two daughters and a son: they were excellent friends. Few couples can say more. The union was good English grey—that of a prolonged November, to which we are reconciled by occasions for the hunt and the gun. She was, nevertheless, an impassioned woman. The feeling for her brother helped to satisfy her heart's fires, though as little with her brother as with her husband was she demonstrative. Lord Ormont disrelished the caresses of relatives.

She, for her part, had so strong a sympathy on behalf of poor gentlemen reduced to submit to any but a young woman's hug, that when, bronzed from India, he quitted the carriage and mounted her steps at Olmer, the desire to fling herself on his neck and breast took form in the words: "Here you are home again, Rowsley; glad to have you." They shook hands firmly.

He remained three days at Olmer. His temper was mild, his frame of mind bad as could be. Angry evaporations had left a residuum of solid scorn for these "English," who rewarded soldierly services as though it were a question of damaged packages of calico. He threatened to take the first offer of a foreign State "not in insurrection." But clear sky was overhead. He was the Rowsley of the old boyish delight in field sports, reminiscences of prowlings and trappings in the woods, gropings along water-banks, enjoyment of racy gossip. He spoke wrathfully of "one of their newspapers" which steadily persisted in withholding from publication every letter he wrote to it, after printing the first. And if it printed one, why not the others?

Lady Charlotte put it on the quaintness of editors.

He had found in London, perhaps, reason for saying that he should do well to be "out of this country" as early as he could; adding, presently, that he meant to go, though "it broke his heart to keep away from a six months' rest at Steignton," his Wiltshire estate.

No woman was in the field. Lady Charlotte could have submitted to the intrusion of one of those at times wholesome victims, for the sake of the mollification the unhappy proud thing might bring to a hero smarting under injustice at the hands of chiefs and authorities.

He passed on to Steignton, returned to London, and left England for Spain, as he wrote word, saying he hoped to settle at Steignton next year. He was absent the next year, and longer. Lady Charlotte had the surprising news that Steignton was let, shooting and all, for five years; and he had no appointment out of England or at home. When he came to Olmer again he was under one of his fits of reserve, best undisturbed. Her sympathy with a great soldier snubbed, an active man rusting, kept her from remonstrance.

Three years later she was made meditative by the discovery of a woman's being absolutely in the field, mistress of the field, and having been there for a considerable period, dating from about the time when he turned his back on England to visit a comrade-in-arms condemned by the doctors to pass the winter in Malaga; and it was a young woman, a girl in her teens, a handsome girl. Handsome was to be expected; Ormont bargained for beauty. But report said the girl was very handsome, and showed breeding: she seemed a foreigner, walked like a Goddess, sat her horse the perfect Amazon. Rumour called her a Spaniard.

"Not if she rides!" Lady Charlotte cut that short.

Rumour had subsequently more to say. The reporter in her ear did not confirm it, and she was resolutely deaf to a story incredible of her brother—the man, of all men living, proudest of his name, blood, station. So proud was he by nature, too, that he disdained to complain of rank injustice; he maintained a cheerful front against adversity and obloquy. And this man of complete self-command, who has every form of noble pride, gets cajoled like a twenty-year-old yahoo at college! Do you imagine it? To suppose of a man cherishing the name of Ormont, that he would bestow it legally on a woman, a stranger, and imperil his race by mixing blood with a creature of unknown lineage, was—why, of course, it was to suppose him struck mad, and there never had been madness among the Ormonts: they were too careful of the purity of the strain. Lady Charlotte talked. She was excited, and ran her sentences to blanks, a cunning way for ministering consolation to her hearing, where the sentence intended a question, and the blank ending caught up the query tone and carried it dwindling away to the most distant of throttled interrogatives. She had, in this manner, only to ask,—her hearing received the comforting answer it desired; for she could take that thin far sound as a travelling laughter of incredulity, triumphant derision.

This meant to her—though she scarcely knew it, though the most wilful of women declined to know it—a state of alarm. She had said of her brother in past days that he would have his time of danger after striking sixty. The dangerous person was to be young.

But, then, Ormont had high principles with regard to the dues to his family. His principles could always be trusted. The dangerous young person would have to be a person of lineage, of a certain station at least: no need for a titled woman, only for warranted good blood. Is that to be found certificated out of the rolls of Society? It may just possibly be found, without certificate, however, in those muddled caverns where the excluded intermingle. Here and there, in a peasant family, or a small country tradesman's just raised above a peasant, honest regenerating blood will be found. Nobles wanting refreshment from the soil might do worse than try a slip of one of those juicy weeds; ill-fated, sickly Royalties would be set-up striding through another half-century with such invigoration, if it could be done for them! There are tales. The tales are honourably discredited by the crazy constitutions of the heirs to the diadem.

Yes, but we are speculating on the matter

seriously, as though it were one of intimate concern to the family. What is there to make us think that Ormont would marry? Impossible to imagine him intimidated. Unlikely that he, a practised reader of women, having so little of the woman in him, would be melted by a wily girl; as women in the twilight situation have often played the trick to come into the bright beams. How? They do a desperate thing, and call it generosity, and then they appeal from it to my lord's generosity; and so the two generosities drive off in a close carriage with a friend and a professional landlady for the blessing of the parson, and are legitimately united. Women have won round fools to give way in that way. And quite right too! thought Lady Charlotte, siding with nature and justice, as she reflected that no woman created would win round her brother to give way in that way. He was too acute. The moment the woman showed sign of becoming an actress, her doom was written. "Poor idiot!" was not uncharitably inscribed by the sisterly lady on the tombstone of hopes aimed with scarce pardonable ambition at her brother.

She blew away the rumour. Ormont, she vowed, had not entitled any woman to share and bear his title. And this was her interpretation of the report: he permitted (if he did permit) the woman to take his name, that he might have a scornful fling at the world maltreating him. Besides, the name was not published, it was not to be seen in the papers; it passed merely among male friends, tradesmen, servants: no great harm in that.

Listen further. Here is an unknown girl: why should he marry her? A girl consenting to the place beside a man of his handsome ripe age, is either bought, or she is madly enamoured; she does not dictate terms. Ormont is not of the brute buyers in that market. One sees it is the girl who leads the dance. A girl is rarely so madly enamoured as when she falls in love with her grandfather; she pitches herself at his head. This had not happened for the first time in Ormont's case; and he had never proposed marriage. Why should he do it now?

But again, if the girl has breeding to some extent, he might think it her due that she should pass under the safeguard of his name, out of sight.

Then, so far the report is trustworthy. We blow the rumour out of belief. A young woman there is: she is not a wife. Lady Charlotte allowed her the fairly respectable post of Hecate of the Shades, as long as the girl was no pretender to the place and name in the upper sphere. Her deductions were plausible, convincing to friends shaken by her vehement manner of coming at them. She convinced herself by means of her multitude of reasons for not pursuing inquiry. Her brother said nothing. There was no need for him to speak. He seemed on one or two occasions in the act of getting himself together for the communication of a secret; and she made ready to listen hard, with ears, eyebrows, shut mouth, and a gleam at the back of her eyes, for a signification of something she would refer him to after he had spoken. He looked at her and held his peace, or virtually held it,—that is, he said not one word on the subject she was to have told him she had anticipated. Lady Charlotte ascribed it to his recollection of the quick blusher, the pained blusher, she was in her girlhood at mention or print of the story of men and women. Who, not having known her, could conceive it! But who could conceive that, behind the positive, plain-dealing, downright woman of the world, there was at times, when a nerve was touched or an old blocked path of imagination thrown open, a sensitive youthfulness, still quick to blush as far as the skin of a grandmother matron might show it!

CHAPTER III.

THE TUTOR.

THERE was no counting now on Lord Ormont's presence in the British gathering seasons, when wheatears wing across our fields or swallows return to their caves. He forsook the hunt to roam the Continent, one of the vulgar band of tourists, honouring town only when May-flies had flown, and London's indiscriminate people went about without their volatile heads.

Lady Charlotte put these changed conditions upon the behaviour of the military authorities to her brother; saying that the wonder was he did not shake the dust of his country from his feet. In her wise head she rejoiced to think he was not the donkey she sketched for admiration; and she was partly consoled, or played at the taking of a comfort needed in her perpetual struggle with a phantom of a fact, by the reflection that a young woman on his arm would cause him to feel himself more at home abroad. Her mind's habit of living warmly beside him in separation was vexed by the fixed intrusion of a female third person, who checked the run of intimate chatter, especially damped the fancied talk over early days—of which the creature was ignorant; and her propinquity to him arrested or broke the dialogue Lady Charlotte invented and pressed to renew. But a wife, while letting him be seen, would have insisted on appropriating the thought of him —all his days, past as well as present. An impassioned sister's jealousy preferred that it should not be a wife reigning to dispute her share of her brother in imagination.

Then came a rumour, telling of him as engaged upon the composition of his Memoirs.

Lady Charlotte's impulsive outcry: "Writing them?" signified her grounds for alarm.

Happily, Memoirs are not among the silly deeds done in a moment; they were somewhere ahead and over the hills: a band of brigands rather than a homely shining mansion, it was true; but distant; and a principal question shrieked to know whether he was composing them for publication. She could look forward with a girl's pleasure to the perusal of them in manuscript, in a woody nook, in a fervour of partisanship, easily avoiding sight of errors, grammatical or moral. She chafed at the possible printing and publishing of them. That would be equivalent to an exhibition of him clean-stripped for a run across London—brilliant in himself, spotty in the offence. Published Memoirs indicate the end of a man's activity, and that he acknowledges the end; and at a period of Lord Ormont's life when the denial of it should thunder. They are his final chapter, making mummy of the grand figure they wrap in the printed stuff. They are virtually his apology. Can those knowing Lord Ormont hear him apologize? But it is a craven apology if we stoop to expound: we are seen as pleading our case before the public. Call it by any name you please, and under any attitude, it is that. And set aside the writing: it may be perfect; the act is the degradation. It is a rousing of swarms. His friends and the public will see the proudest nobleman of his day, pleading his case in mangled English, in the headlong of an outpoured, undrilled, rabble vocabulary, doubling the ridicule by his imperturbability over the ridicule he excites: he who is no more ridiculous, cried the partisan sister, conjuring up the scene, not an ace more ridiculous, than a judge of assize calling himself miserable sinner on Sunday before the parson, after he has very properly condemned half-a-score of weekday miserable sinners to penal servitude or the rope. Nobody laughs at the judge. Everybody will be laughing at the scornful man down half-way to his knee-caps with a stutter of an apology for having done his duty to his country, after stigmatizing numbers for inability or ill-will to do it. But Ormont's weapon is the sword, not a pen! Lady Charlotte hunted her simile till the dogs had it or it ran to earth.

She struck at the conclusion, that the young woman had been persuading him. An adoring young woman is the person to imagine and induce to the commission of such folly. "What do you think? You have seen her, you say?" she asked of a man she welcomed for his flavour of the worldling's fine bile.

Lord Adderwood made answer: "She may be having a hand in it. She worships, and that is your way of pulling gods to the ground."

"Does she understand good English?"

"Speaks it."

"Can she write?"

"I have never had a letter from her."

"You tell me Morsfield admires the woman—would marry her to-morrow, if he could get her."

"He would go through the ceremony Ormont has performed, I do not doubt."

"I don't doubt all of you are ready. She doesn't encourage one?"

"On the contrary, all."

"She's clever. This has been going on for now seven years, and, as far as I know, she has my brother fast."

"She may have done the clever trick of having him fast from the beginning."

"She'd like people to think it."

"She has an aunt to advertise it."

"Ormont can't swallow the woman, I'm told."

"Trying, if one is bound to get her down!"

"Boasts of the connection everywhere she's admitted, Randeller says."

"Randeller procures the admission to various parti-coloured places."

"She must be a blinking moll-owl! And I ask any sane Christian or Pagan—proof enough!—would my brother Rowsley let his wife visit those places, those people? Monstrous to have the suspicion that he would, if you know him! Mrs. Lawrence Finchley, for example. I say nothing to hurt the poor woman; I back her against her imbecile of a husband. He brings a charge he can't support; she punishes him by taking three years' lease of independence, and kicks up the grass all over the paddock, and then comes cuckoo, barking his name abroad to have her home again. You can win the shyest filly to corn at last. She goes, and he digests ruefully the hotchpotch of a dish the woman brings him. Only the world spies a side-head at her, husbanded or not, though the main fault was his, and she had a right to insist that he should be sure of his charge before he smacked her in the face with it before the world. In dealing with a woman, a man commonly prudent—put aside chivalry, justice, and the rest—should bind himself to disbelieve what he can't prove. Otherwise, let him expect his whipping, with or without ornament. My opinion is, Lawrence Finchley had no solid foundation for his charge, except his being an imbecile. She wasn't one of the adventurous women to jump the bars,—the gate had to be pushed open, and he did it. There she is; and I ask you, would my brother Rowsley let his *wife* be intimate with her? And there are others. And, *sauf votre respect*, the men—Morsfield for one, Randeller another!"

"They have a wholesome dread of the lion."

"If they smell a chance with the lion's bone—it's the sweeter for being the lion's. These metaphors carry us off our ground. I must let these Ormont Memoirs run and upset him, if they get to print. I've only to oppose, printed they'll be. The same if I say a word of this woman, he marries her to-morrow morning. You speak of my driving men. Why can't I drive Ormont? Because I'm too fond of him. There you have the secret of the subjection of women: they can hold their own, and a bit more, when they've no enemy beating inside."

"Hearts!—ah, well, it's possible. I don't

say no; I've not discovered them," Lord Adderwood observed.

They are rarely discovered in the haunts he frequented.

Her allusion to Mrs. Lawrence Finchley rapped him smartly, and she admired his impassiveness under the stroke. Such a spectacle was one of her pleasures.

Lady Charlotte mentioned incidentally her want of a tutor for her grandson Leo during the winter holidays. He suggested an application to the clergyman of her parish. She was at feud with the Rev. Stephen Hampton-Evey, and would not take, she said, a man to be a bootblack in her backyard or a woman a scullery-wench in her kitchen upon his recommendation. She described the person of Mr. Hampton-Evey, his manner of speech, general opinions, professional doctrines; rolled him into a ball and bowled him, with a shrug for lamentation over the decay of the good old order of manly English Protestant clergymen, who drank their port, bothered nobody about belief, abstained from preaching their sermon, if requested; were capital fellows in the hunting-field, too; for if they came, they had the spur to hunt in the devil's despite. Now we are going to have a kind of bitter, clawed, forked female, in vestments over breeches. "How do you like that bundling of the sexes?"

Lord Adderwood liked the lines of division to be strictly and invitingly definite. He was thinking, as he reviewed the frittered appearance of the Rev. Stephen Hampton-Evey in Lady Charlotte's hands, of the possibility that Lord Ormont, who was reputed to fear nobody, feared her. In which case, the handsome young woman passing among his associates as the pseudo Lady Ormont might be the real one after all, and Isabella Lawrence Finchley prove right in the warning she gave to dogs of chase.

The tutor required by Lady Charlotte was found for her by Mr. Abner. Their correspondence on the subject filled the space of a week, and then the gentleman hired to drive a creaky wheel came down from London to Olmer, arriving late in the evening.

Lady Charlotte's blunt "Oh!" when he entered her room and bowed upon the announcement of his name, was caused by an instantaneous perception and reflection that it would be prudent to keep her granddaughter Philippa, aged between seventeen and eighteen, out of his way.

"You are a friend of Mr. Abner's, are you?"

He was not disconcerted. He replied, in an assured and pleasant voice, "I have hardly the pretension to be called a friend, madam."

"Are you a Jew?"

Her abruptness knocked something like a

laugh almost out of him, but he restrained the signs of it.

"I am not."

"You wouldn't be ashamed to tell me you were one if you were?"

"Not at all."

"You like the Jews?"

"Those I know I like."

"Not many Christians have the good sense and the good heart of Arthur Abner. Now go and eat. Come back to me when you've done. I hope you are hungry. Ask the butler for the wine you prefer."

She had not anticipated the enrolment in her household of a man so young and good-looking. These were qualifications for Cupid's business, which his unstrained self-possession accentuated to a note of danger to her chicks, because she liked the taste of him. Her grand-daughter Philippa was in the girl's waxen age; another, Beatrice, was coming to it. Both were under her care;

and she was a vigilant woman, with an intuition and a knowledge of sex. She did not blame Arthur Abner for sending her a good-looking young man; she had only a general idea that tutors in a house, and even visiting tutors, should smell of dust and wear a snuffy appearance. The conditions will not always insure the tutors from foolishness, as her girl's experience reminded her, but they protect the girl.

"Your name is Weyburn; your father was an officer in the army, killed on the battle-field, Arthur Abner tells me," was her somewhat severely-toned greeting to the young tutor on his presenting himself the second time.

It had the sound of the preliminary of an indictment read in a Court of Law.

"My father died of his wounds in hospital," he said.

"Why did you not enter the service?"

"Want of an income, my lady."

"Bad look-out. Army or Navy for gentlemen, if they stick to the school of honour. The sedentary professions corrupt men: bad for the blood. Those monastery monks found that out. They had to birch the devil out of them three times a day and half the night, howling like full-moon dogs all through their lives, till the flesh was off them. That was their exercise, if they were for holiness. My brother, Lord Ormont, has never been still in his youth or his manhood. See him now. He counts his years by scores; and he has about as many wrinkles as you when you're smiling. His cheeks are as red as yours now you're blushing. You ought to have left off that trick by this time. It's well enough in a boy."

Against her will she was drawn to the young man, and her consciousness of it plucked her back to caution with occasional jerks—quaint alternations of the familiar and the harshly formal in the stranger's experience.

"If I have your permission, Lady Charlotte," said he, "the reason why I mounted a little—if I do it—is, you mention Lord Ormont, and I have followed his career since I was the youngest of boys."

"Good to begin with the worship of a hero. He can't sham, can't deceive—not even a woman; and you're old enough to understand the temptation: they're so silly. All the more, it's a point of honour with a man of honour to shield her from herself. When it's a girl——"

The young man's eyebrows bent.

"Chapters of stories, if you want to hear them," she resumed; "and I can vouch some of them true. Lord Ormont was never one of the wolves in a hood. Whatever you hear of him, you may be sure he laid no trap. He's just the opposite to the hypocrite; so hypocrites hate him. I've heard them called high-priests of decency. Then we choose to be indecent and honest, if there's a God to worship. Fear, they're in the habit of saying—we are to fear God. A man here, a Rev. Hampton-Evey, you'll hear him harp on 'fear God.' Hypocrites may: honest sinners have no fear. And see the cause: they don't deceive themselves —that is why. Do you think we can love what we fear? They love God, or they disbelieve. And if they believe in Him, they know they can't conceal anything from Him. Honesty means piety: we can't be one without the other. And here are people—parsons—who talk of dying as *going* into the presence of our Maker, as if He had been all the while outside the world He created. Those parsons, I told the Rev. Hampton-Evey here, make infidels—they make a puzzle of their God. I'm for a rational Deity. They preach up a supernatural eccentric. I don't say all: I've heard good sermons, and met sound-headed clergymen—not like that gaping Hampton-Evey, when a woman tells him she thinks for herself. We have him sitting on our parish. A free-thinker startles him as a kind of demon; but a female free-thinker is one of Satan's concubines. He took it upon himself to reproach me—flung his glove at my feet, because I sent a cheque to a poor man punished for blasphemy. The man had the right to his opinions, and he had the courage of his opinions. I doubt whether the Rev. Hampton-Evey would go with a willing heart to prison for his. All the better for him if he comes head-up out of a trial. But now see: all these parsons and judges and mobcaps insist upon conformity. A man with common manly courage comes before them, and he's cast in penalties. Yet we know from history, in England, France, Germany, that the time of nonconformity brought out the manhood of the nation. Now, I say, a nation, to be a nation, must have men—I mean brave men. That's what those hosts of female men combine to try to stifle. They won't succeed, but we shall want a war to teach the country the value of courage. You catch what I am driving at? They accuse my brother of immorality because he makes no pretence to be better than the men of his class."

Weyburn's eyelids fluttered. Her kite-like ascent into the general, with the sudden drop on her choice morsel, switched his humour at the moment when he was respectfully considering that her dartings and gyrations had motive as much as the flight of the swallow for food. They had meaning; and here was one of the great ladies of the land who thought for herself, and was thoughtful for the country. If she came down like a bird winged, it was her love of her brother that did it. His look at Lady Charlotte glistened.

She raised her defences against the basilisk fascinating Philippa; and with a vow to keep them apart and deprive him of his chance, she relapsed upon the stiff frigidity which was not natural to her. It lasted long enough to put him on his guard under the seductions of a noble dame's condescension to a familiar tone. But, as he was too well bred to show the change in his mind for her change of manner, and as she was the sister of his boyhood's hero, and could be full of flavour, his eyes retained something of their sparkle. They were ready to lighten again, in the way peculiar to him, when she, quite forgetting her defence of Philippa, disburdened herself of her antagonisms and enthusiasms, her hates and her loves all round the neighbourhood and over the world, won to confidential communication by this young man's face. She confessed as much, had he been guided to perceive it. She said, " Arthur Abner's a reader of men: I can trust his word about them."

Presently, it is true, she added: "No man's to be relied upon where there's a woman." She refused her implicit trust to saints—"if ever a man really was a saint before he was canonized!"

Her penetrative instinct of sex kindled the scepticism. Sex she saw at play everywhere, dogging the conduct of affairs, directing them at times; she saw it as the animation of nature, senselessly stigmatized, hypocritically concealed, active in our thoughts where not in our deeds; and the declining of the decorous to see it, or admit the sight, got them abhorred bad names from her, after a touch at the deadly poison coming of that blindness, or blindfoldedness, and a grimly melancholy shrug over the cruelties resulting—cruelties chiefly affecting women.

"You're too young to have thought upon

such matters," she said, for a finish to them.

That was hardly true.

"I have thought," said Weyburn, and his head fell to reckoning of the small sum of his thoughts upon them.

He was pulled up instantly for close inspection by the judge. "What is your age?"

"I am in my twenty-sixth year."

"You have been among men: have you studied women?"

"Not largely, Lady Charlotte. Opportunity has been wanting at French and German colleges."

"It's only a large and a close and a pretty long study of them that can teach you anything; and you must get rid of the poetry about them, and be sure you haven't lost it altogether. That's what is called the golden mean. I'm not for the golden mean in every instance; it's a way of exhorting to brutal selfishness. I grant it's the right way in those questions. You'll learn in time." Her scanning gaze at the young man's face drove him along an avenue of his very possible chances of learning. "Certain to. But don't tell me that at your age you have thought about women. You may say you have felt. A young man's feelings about women are better reading for him six or a dozen chapters further on. Then he can sift and strain. It won't be perfectly clear, but it will do."

Mr. Eglett hereupon threw the door open, and ushered in Master Leo.

Lady Charlotte noticed that the tutor shook the boy's hand offhandedly, with not a whit of the usual obtrusive geniality, and merely dropped him a word. Soon after, he was talking to Mr. Eglett of games at home and games abroad. Poor fun over there! We head the world in field games, at all events. He drew a picture of a foreigner of his acquaintance looking on at football. On the other hand, French boys and German, having passed a year or two at an English school, get the liking for our games, and do a lot of good when they go home. The things we learn from them are to dance, to sing, and to study :—they are more in earnest than we about study. They teach us at fencing too. The tutor praised fencing as an exercise and an accomplishment. He had large reserves of eulogy for boxing. He knew the qualities of the famous bruisers of the time, cited fisty names, whose owners were then to be seen all over an admiring land in prints, in the glorious defensive-offensive attitude, England's own—Touch me, if you dare! with bullish, or bull-dog, or oak-bole fronts for the blow, handsome to pugilistic eyes.

The young tutor had lighted on a pet theme of Mr Eglett's—the excelling virtues of the practice of pugilism in Old England,

and the school of honour that it is to our lower population. " Fifty times better for them than cock-fighting," he exclaimed, admitting that he could be an interested spectator at a ring or the pit: cock-fighting or ratting.

"Ratting seems to have more excuse," the tutor said, and made no sign of a liking for either of those popular pastimes. As he disapproved without squeamishness, the impulsive but sharply critical woman close by nodded; and she gave him his dues for being no courtier.

Leo had to be off to bed. The tutor spared him any struggle over the shaking of hands, and saying, "Good-night, Leo," continued the conversation. The boy went away visibly relieved of the cramp that seizes on a youngster at the formalities pertaining to these chilly and fateful introductions.

" What do you think of the look of him?" Mr. Eglett asked.

The tutor had not appeared to inspect the boy. "Big head," he remarked. "Yes, Leo won't want pushing at books when he's once in harness. He will have six weeks of me. It's more than the yeomanry get for drill per annum, and they're expected to know something of a soldier's duties. There's a chance of putting him on the right road in certain matters. We'll walk, or ride, or skate, if the frost holds to-morrow: no lessons the first day."

"Do as you think fit," said Lady Charlotte.

The one defect she saw in the tutor did not concern his pupil. And a girl, if hit, would be unable to see that this tutor, judged as a man, was to some extent despicable for accepting tutorships, and, one might say, dishonouring the family of a soldier of rank and distinction, by coming into houses at the back way, with footing enough to air his graces when once established there. He ought to have knocked at every door in the kingdom for help, rather than accept tutorships, and disturb households (or providently-minded mistresses of them) with all sorts of probably groundless apprehensions, founded naturally enough on the good looks he intrudes.

This tutor committed the offence next day of showing he had a firm and easy seat in the saddle, which increased Lady Charlotte's liking for him and irritated her watchful forecasts. She rode with the young man after lunch, "to show him the country," and gave him a taste of what he took for her variable moods. He misjudged her. Like a swimmer going through warm and cold springs of certain lake waters, he thought her a capricious ladyship, dangerous for intimacy, alluring to the deeps and gripping with cramps.

She pushed him to defend his choice of the tutor's profession.

"Think you understand boys?" she caught up his words; "you can't. You can humour them, as you humour women. They're just as hard to read. And don't tell me a young man can read women. Boys and women go on their instincts. Egyptologists can spell you hieroglyphs; they'd be stumped, as Leo would say, to read a spider out of an ink-pot over a sheet of paper."

"One gets to interpret by degrees, by observing their habits," the tutor said, and vexed her with a towering complacency under provocation that went some way further to melt the woman she was, while her knowledge of the softness warned her still more of the duty of playing dragon round such a young man in her house. The despot is alert at every issue, to every chance; and she was one, the wakefuller for being benevolent; her mind had no sleep by day.

For a month she subjected Mr. Matthew Weyburn to the microscope of her observation and the probe of her instinct. He proved that he could manage without cajoling a boy. The practical fact established, by agreement between herself and the unobservant gentleman who was her husband, Lady Charlotte allowed her meditations to drop an indifferent glance at the speculative views upon education entertained by this young tutor. To her mind they were flighty; but she liked him, and as her feelings dictated to her mind when she had not to think for others, she spoke of his views toleratingly, almost with an implied approval, after passing them through the form of burlesque to which she customarily treated things failing to waft her enthusiasm. In regard to Philippa, he behaved well: he bestowed more of his attention on Beatrice, nearer Leo's age, in talk about games and storybooks and battles; nothing that he did when the girls were present betrayed the strutting plumed cock, bent to attract, or the sickly reptile, thirsty for a prize above him and meaning to have it, like Satan in Eden. Still, of course, he could not help his being a handsome fellow, having a vivid face and eyes transparent, whether blue or green, to flame of the brain exciting them; and that becomes a picture in the dream of girls—a picture creating the dream often. And Philippa had asked her grandmother, very ingenuously indeed, with a most natural candour, why " they saw so little of Leo's hero." Simple female child!

However, there was no harm done, and Lady Charlotte liked him. She liked few. Forthwith, in the manner of her particular head, a restless head, she fell to work at combinations.

Thus :—he is a nice young fellow, well-bred, no cringing courtier, accomplished, good at classics, fairish at mathematics, a scholar in French, German, Italian, with a shrewd knowledge of the different races, and with sound English sentiment too, and the capacity for writing good English, although in those views of his the ideas are unusual, therefore un-English, profoundly so. But his intentions are patriotic; they would not displease Lord Ormont. He has a worship of Lord Ormont. All we can say on behalf of an untried inferior is in that,— only the valiant admire devotedly. Well, he can write grammatical, readable English. What if Lord Ormont were to take him as a secretary while the Memoirs are in hand? He might help to chasten the sentences laughed at by those newspapers. Or he might, being a terrible critic of writing, and funny about styles, put it in an absurd light, that would cause the Memoirs to be tossed into the fire. He was made for the post of secretary! The young man's good looks would be out of harm's way then. If any sprig of womankind come across him there, it will, at any rate, not be a girl. Women must take care of themselves. Only the fools among them run to mischief in the case of a handsome young fellow.

Supposing a certain woman to be one of the fools? Lady Charlotte merely suggested it in the dashing current of her meditations—did not strike it out interrogatively. The woman would be a fine specimen among her class; that was all. For the favourite of Lord Ormont to stoop from her place beside him ―― ay, but women do; heroes have had the woeful experience of that fact. First we see them aiming themselves at their hero; next they are shooting an eye at the handsome man. The thirst of nature comes after that of their fancy, in conventional women. Sick of the hero tried, tired of their place in the market, no longer ashamed to acknowledge it, they begin to consult their own taste for beauty—they have it quite as much as the men have it; and when their worshipped figure of manliness, in a romantic sombrero, is a threadbare giant, showing bruises, they sink on their inherent desire for a dance with the handsome man. And the really handsome man is the most extraordinary of the rarities. No wonder that when he appears he slays them, walks over them like a pestilence!

This young Weyburn would touch the fancy of a woman of a romantic turn. Supposing her enthusiastic in her worship of the hero, after a number of years—for anything may be imagined where a woman is concerned—why, another enthusiasm for the same object, and on the part of a stranger, a stranger with effective eyes, rapidly leads to sympathy. Suppose the reverse—the enthusiasm gone to dust, or become a wheezy old bellows, as it does where there's disparity of age, or it frequently does—then the sympathy with a good-looking stranger comes more rapidly still.

These were Lady Charlotte's glances right and left—idle flights of the eye of a mounted Amazon across hedges at the canter along the main road of her scheme; which was to do a service to the young man she liked and to the brother she loved, for the marked advantage of both equally; perhaps for the chance of a little gossip to follow about that tenacious woman by whom her brother was held hard and fast, kept away from friends and relatives, isolated, insomuch as to have given up living on his estate—the old home!—because he would not disgrace it or incur odium by taking her there.

In consequence of Lord Ormont's resistance

to pressure from her on two or three occasions, she chose to nurse and be governed by the maxim for herself: Never propose a plan to him, if you want it adopted. That was her way of harmlessly solacing love's vindictiveness for an injury.

She sent Arthur Abner a letter, thanking him for his recommendation of young Mr. Weyburn, stating her benevolent wishes as regarded the young man and "those hateful Memoirs," requesting that her name should not be mentioned in the affair, because she was anxious on all grounds to have the proposal accepted by her brother. She could have vowed to herself that she wrote sincerely. "He must want a secretary. He would be shy at an offer of one from me. Do you hint it, if you get a chance. You gave us Mr. Weyburn, and Mr. Eglett and I like him. Ormont would too, I am certain. You have obliged him before; this will be better than anything you have done for us. It will stop the Memoirs, or else give them a polish. Your young friend has made me laugh over stuff taken for literature until we put on our spectacles. Leo jogs along in harness now, and may do some work at school yet."

Having posted her letter, she left the issue to chance, as we may when conscience is easy. An answer came the day before Weyburn's departure. Arthur Abner had met Lord Ormont in the street, had spoken of the rumour of Memoirs promised to the world, hinted at the possible need for a secretary; "Lord Ormont would appoint a day to see Mr. Weyburn."

Lady Charlotte considered that to be as good as the engagement.

"So we keep you in the family," she said. "And now look here: you ought to know my brother's ways, if you're going to serve him. You'll have to guess at half of everything he tells you; he'll expect you to know the whole. There's no man so secret. Why? he fears nothing. I can't tell why. And what his mouth shuts on, he exposes as if in his hand. Of course he's proud, and good reason. You'll see when you mustn't offend. A lady's in the house—I hear of it. She takes his name, they say. She may be a respectable woman—I've heard no scandal. We have to hear of a Lady Ormont out of Society! We have to suppose it means there's not to be a real one. He can't marry if he has allowed her to go about bearing his name. She has a fool of an aunt, I'm told; as often in the house as not. Good proof of his fondness for the woman, if he swallows half a year of the aunt! Well, you won't, unless you've mere man's eyes, be able to help seeing him trying to hide what he suffers from that aunt. He bears it, like the man he is; but woe to another betraying it! She has a tongue that goes like the reel of a rod, with a pike bolting out of the shallows to the snag he knows—to wind round it and defy you to pull. Often my brother Rowsley and I have fished the day long, and in hard weather, and brought home a basket; and he boasted of it more than of anything he has ever done since. That woman holds him away from me now. I say no harm of her. She may be right enough from her point of view; or it mayn't be owing to her. I wouldn't blame a woman. Well, but my point with you is, you swallow the woman's aunt—the lady's aunt—without betraying you suffer at all. Lord Ormont has eyes of an eagle for a speck above the surface. All the more because the aunt is a gabbling idiot does he—I say it seeing it—fire up to defend her from the sneer of the lip or half a sign of it! No, you would be on your guard; I can trust you. Of course you'd behave like the gentleman you are where any kind of woman's concerned; but you mustn't let a shadow be seen, think what you may. The woman—lady—calling herself Lady Ormont,—poor woman, I should do the same in her place,—she has a hard game to play; I have to be for my family: she has manners, I'm told; holds herself properly. She fancies she brings him up to the altar, in the end, by decent behaviour. That's a delusion. It's creditable to her, only she can't understand the claims of the family upon a man like my brother. When you have spare time—'kick-ups,' he used to call it, writing to me from school—come here; you're welcome, after three days' notice. I shall be glad to see you again. You've gone some way to make a man of Leo."

He liked her well: he promised to come. She was a sinewy bite of the gentle sex, but she had much flavour, and she gave nourishment.

"Let me have three days' notice," she repeated.

"Not less, Lady Charlotte," said he.

Weyburn received intimation from Arthur Abner of the likely day Lord Ormont would appoint, and he left Olmer for London to hold himself in readiness. Lady Charlotte and Leo drove him to meet the coach. Philippa, so strangely baffled in her natural curiosity, begged for a seat; she begged to be allowed to ride. Petitions were rejected. She stood at the window seeing "Grandmama's tutor," as she named him, carried off by grandmama. Her nature was avenged on her tyrant grandmama: it brought up almost to her tongue thoughts which would have remained subterranean, under control of her habit of mind, or the nursery's modesty, if she had been less tyrannically treated.

They were subterranean thoughts, Nature's original, such as the sense of injustice will rouse in young women; and they are better unstirred, for they ripen girls over-rapidly when they are made to revolve near the surface. It flashed on the girl why she had been treated tyrannically.

"Grandmama has good taste in tutors," was all that she said while the thoughts rolled over.

CHAPTER IV.

RECOGNITION.

Our applicant for the post of secretary entered the street of Lord Ormont's London house, to present himself to his boyhood's hero by appointment.

He was to see, perhaps to serve, the great soldier. Things had come to this; and he thought it singular. But for the previous introduction to Lady Charlotte, he would have thought it passing wonderful. He ascribed it to the whirligig.

The young man was not yet of an age to gather knowledge of himself and of life from his present experience of the fact, that passionate devotion to an object strikes a vein through circumstances, as a travelling run of flame darts the seeming haphazard zigzags to catch at the dry of dead wood amid the damp; and when passion has become quiescent in the admirer, there is often the unsubsided first impulsion carrying it on. He will almost surely embrace his idol with one or other of the senses.

Weyburn still read the world as it came to him, by bits, marvelling at this and that, after the fashion of most of us. He had not deserted his adolescent's hero, or fallen upon analysis of a past season. But he was now a young man, stoutly and cognizantly on the climb, with a good aim overhead, and green youth's enthusiasms a step below his heels: one of the lovers of life, beautiful to behold, when we spy into them; generally their aspect is an enlivenment, whatever may be the carving of their features. For. the sake of holy unity, this lover of life, whose gaze was to the front in hungry animation, held fast to his young dreams, perceiving a soul of meaning in them, though the fire might have gone out; and he confessed to a past pursuit of delusions. Young men of this kind will have, for the like reason, a similar rational sentiment on behalf of our world's historic forward march, while admitting that history has to be taken from far backward if we would gain assurance of man's advance. It nerves an admonished ambition.

He was ushered into a London house's library, looking over a niggard enclosure of gravel and dull grass, against a wall where ivy dribbled. An arm-chair was beside the fire-place. To right and left of it a floreate company of books in high cases paraded shoulder to shoulder, without a gap, grenadiers on the line. Weyburn read the titles on their scarlet-and-blue facings. They were approved English classics; honoured veterans, who have emerged from the conflict with contemporary opinion, stamped excellent, or have been pushed by the roar of contemporaneous applauses to wear the leather-and-gilt uniform of our Immortals, until a more qualmish posterity disgorges them. The books had costly bindings. Lord Ormont's treatment of literature appeared to resemble Lady Charlotte's, in being reverential and uninquiring. The books she bought to read were Memoirs of her time by dead men and women once known to her. These did fatigue duty in cloth or undress. It was high drill with all of Lord Ormont's books, and there was not a modern or a minor name among the regiments. They smelt strongly of the bookseller's lump lots by order; but if a show soldiery, they were not a sham, like a certain row of venerably-titled backs, that Lady Charlotte, without scruple, left standing to blow an ecclesiastical trumpet of empty contents; any one might have his battle of brains with them, for the turning of an absent key.

The door opened. Weyburn bowed to his old star in human shape: a grey head on square shoulders, filling the doorway. He had seen at Olmer Lady Charlotte's treasured miniature portrait of her brother; a perfect likeness, she said—complaining the next instant of injustice done to the fire of his look.

Fire was low down behind the eyes at present. They were quick to scan and take summary of their object, as the young man felt while observing for himself. Height and build of body were such as might be expected in the brother of Lady Charlotte and from the tales of his prowess. Weyburn had a glance back at Cuper's boys listening to the tales.

The soldier-lord's manner was courteously military—that of an established superior indifferent to the deferential attitude he must needs exact. His curt nick of the head, for a response to the visitor's formal salutation, signified the requisite acknowledgment, like a city creditor's busy stroke of the type-stamp receipt upon payment.

The ceremony over, he pitched a bugle voice to fit the contracted area: "I hear from Mr. Abner that you have made acquaintance with Olmer. Good hunting country there."

"Lady Charlotte kindly gave me a mount, my lord."

"I knew your father by name—Colonel Sidney Weyburn. You lost him at Toulouse. We were in the Peninsula; I was at Talavera with him. Bad day for our cavalry."

"Our officers were young at their work then."

"They taught the Emperor's troops to respect a charge of English horse. It was teaching their fox to set traps for them."

Lord Ormont indicated a chair. He stood.

"The French had good cavalry leaders," Weyburn said, for cover to a continued study of the face.

"Montbrun, yes; Murat, Lassalle, Bessières. Under the Emperor they had."

"You think them not at home in the saddle, my lord?"

"Frenchmen have nerves; horses *are* nerves. They pile excitement too high. When cool, they're among the best. None of them had head for command of all the arms."

"One might say the same of Seidlitz and Ziethen?"

"Of Ziethen. Seidlitz had a wider grasp, I suppose." He pursed his mouth, pondering. "No; and in the Austrian service, too; generals of cavalry are left to whistle for an independent command. There's a jealousy of our branch!" The injured warrior frowned and hummed. He spoke his thought mildly: "Jealousy of the name of soldier in this country! Out of the service is the place to recommend. I'd have advised a son of mine to train for a jockey rather than enter it. We deal with that to-morrow, in my papers. You come to me? Mr. Abner has arranged the terms? So I see you at ten in the morning. I am glad to meet a young man—Englishman—who takes an interest in the service."

Weyburn fancied the hearing of a step; he heard the whispering dress. It passed him; a lady went to the arm-chair. She took her seat, as she had moved, with sedateness, the exchange of a toneless word with my lord. She was a *brune*. He saw that when he rose to do homage.

Lord Ormont resumed: "Some are born to it, must be soldiers; and in peace they are snubbed by the heads; in war they are abused by the country. They don't understand in England how to treat an army; how to make one either!

"The gentleman—Mr. Weyburn: Mr. Arthur Abner's recommendation," he added, hurriedly, with a light wave of his hand and a murmur, that might be the lady's title; continuing: "A young man of military tastes should take service abroad. They're in earnest about it over there. Here they play at it; and an army's shipped to land without commissariat, ambulances, medical stores, and march against the odds, as usual—if it can march!"

"Albuera, my lord?"

"Our men can spurt, for a flick o' the whip. They're expected to be constantly ready for doing prodigies—to repair the country's omissions. All the country cares for is to hope Dick Turpin may get to York. Our men are good beasts; they give the best in 'em, and drop. More's the scandal to a country that has grand material and overtasks it. A blazing disaster ends the chapter!"

This was talk of an injured veteran. It did not deepen the hue of his ruddied skin. He spoke in the tone of matter of fact. Weyburn had been prepared for something of the sort by his friend, Arthur Abner. He noted the speaker's heightened likeness under excitement to Lady Charlotte. Excitement came at an early call of their voices to both; and both had handsome, open features, bluntly cut, nothing of aquiline or the supercilious; eyes bluish-grey, in arched recesses, horny between the thick lids, lively to shoot their meaning when the trap-mouth was active; effectively expressing promptitude for combat, pleasure in attack, wrestle, tug, whatever pertained to strife; an absolute sense of their right.

As there was a third person present at this discussion of military topics, the silence of the lady drew Weyburn to consult her opinion in her look.

It was on him. Strange are the woman's eyes which can unoffendingly assume the privilege to dwell on such a living object as a man without becoming gateways for his return look, and can seem in pursuit of thoughts while they enfold. They were large dark eyes, eyes of southern night. They sped no shot; they rolled forth an envelopment. A child among toys, caught to think of other toys, may gaze in that way. But these were a woman's eyes.

He gave Lord Ormont his whole face, as an auditor should. He was interested besides, as he told a ruffled conscience. He fell upon the study of his old hero determinedly.

The pain of a memory waking under pillows, unable to do more than strain for breath, distracted his attention. There was a memory: that was all he knew. Or else he would have lashed himself for hanging on the beautiful eyes of a woman. To be seeing and hearing his old hero was wonder enough.

Recollections of Lady Charlotte's plain hints regarding the lady present resolved to the gross retort, that her eyes were beautiful. And he knew them—there lay the strangeness. They were known beautiful eyes, in a foreign land of night and mist.

Lord Ormont was discoursing with racy eloquence of our hold on India: his views in which respect were those of Cuper's boys. Weyburn ventured a dot-running description of the famous ride, and out flew an English soldier's grievance. But was not the unjustly-treated great soldier well rewarded, whatever the snubs and the bitterness, with these large dark eyes in his house, for his own? Eyes like these are the beginning of a young man's world; they nerve, inspire, arm him, colour his life; he would labour, fight, die for them. It seemed to Weyburn a blessedness even to behold them. So it had been with him at the early stage; and his heart went swifter, memory fetched a breath. Memory quivered eyelids, when the thought returned—of his having known eyes as lustrous. First lights of his world, they had more volume, warmth, mystery—were sweeter. Still, these in the room were sisters to them. They quickened throbs; they seemed a throb of the heart made visible.

That was their endowment of light and lustre simply, and the mystical curve of the lids. For so they could look only because the heart was disengaged from them. They were but heavenly orbs.

The lady's elbow was on an arm of her chair, her forefinger at her left temple. Her mind was away, one might guess;

she could hardly be interested in talk of soldiering and of foreign army systems, jealous English authorities and officials, games, field-sports. She had personal matters to think of.

Adieu until to-morrow to the house she inhabited! The street was a banishment and a relief when Weyburn's first interview with Lord Ormont was over.

He rejoiced to tell his previous anticipations that he had not been disappointed; and he bade hero-worshippers expect no gilded figure. We gather heroes as we go, if we are among the growing: our constancy is shown in the not discarding of our old ones. He held to his earlier hero, though he had seen him, and though he could fancy he saw round him.

Another, too, had been a hero-lover. How did that lady of night's eyes come to fall into her subjection?

He put no question as to the name she

bore; it hung in a black suspense—vividly at its blackest illuminated her possessor. A man is a hero to some effect who wins a woman like this; and, if his glory bespells her, so that she flings all to the winds for him, burns the world; if, for solely the desperate rapture of belonging to him, she consents of her free will to be one of the nameless and discoloured, he shines in a way to make the marrow of men thrill with a burning envy. For that must be the idolatrous devotion desired by them all.

Weyburn struck down upon his man's nature—the bad in us, when beauty of woman is viewed; or say, the old original revolutionary, best kept untouched; for a touch or a meditative pause above him, fetches him up to roam the civilized world devouringly and lawlessly. It is the special peril of the young lover of life, that an inflammability to beauty in women is at a breath intense with him. He is, in truth, a thinly-sealed volcano of our imperishable ancient father, and has it in him to be the multitudinously-amorous of the mythologic Jove. Give him head, he can be civilization's devil. Is she fair and under a shade?—then is she doubly fair. The shadow about her secretes mystery, just as the forest breeds romance: and mystery is a measureless realm. If we conceive it, we have a mysterious claim on her who is the heart of it.

He marched on that road to the music of sonorous brass for some drunken minutes.

The question came, What of the man who takes advantage of her self-sacrifice?

It soon righted him, and he did Lord Ormont justice, and argued the case against Lady Charlotte's naked hints.

This dark-eyed heroine's bearing was assured, beyond an air of dependency. Her deliberate short nod to him at his leave-taking, and the toneless few words she threw to my lord, signified sufficiently that she did not stand defying the world or dreading it.

She had by miracle the eyes which had once charmed him—could again—would always charm. She reminded him of Aminta Farrell's very eyes under the couchant-dove brows—something of her mouth, the dimple running from a corner. She had, as Aminta had, the self-collected and self-cancelled look, a realm in a look, that was neither depth nor fervour, nor a bestowal, nor an allurement; nor was it an exposure, though there seemed no reserve. One would be near the meaning in declaring it to bewilder men with the riddle of open-handedness. We read it—all may read it —as we read inexplicable plain life; in which let us have a confiding mind, despite the blows at our heart, and some understanding will enter us.

He shut the door upon picture and speculations, returning to them by another door. The lady had not Aminta's freshness: she might be taken for an elder sister of Aminta. But Weyburn wanted to have her position defined before he set her beside Aminta. He writhed under Lady Charlotte's tolerating scorn of "the young woman." It roused an uneasy sentiment of semi-hostility in the direction of my lord; and he had no personal complaint to make.

Lord Ormont was cordial on the day of the secretary's installation; as if—if one might dare to guess it—some one had helped him to a friendly judgement.

The lady of Aminta's eyes was absent at the luncheon table. She came into the room a step, to speak to Lord Ormont, dressed for a drive to pay a visit.

The secretary was unnoticed.

Lord Ormont put inquiries to him at

table, for the why of his having avoided the profession of arms; and apparently considered that the secretary had made a mistake, and that he would have committed a greater error in becoming a soldier—" in this country." A man with a grievance is illogical under his burden. He mentioned the name "Lady Ormont" distinctly during some remarks on travel. Lady Ormont preferred the Continent.

Two days later she came to the arm-chair, as before, met Weyburn's eyes when he raised them; gave him no home in hers—not a temporary shelter from the pelting of interrogations. She hardly spoke. Why did she come?

But how was it that he was drawn to think of her? Absent or present, she was round him, like the hills of a valley. She was round his thoughts—caged them; however high, however far they flew, they were conscious of her.

She took her place at the midday meal. She had Aminta's voice in some tones; a mellower than Aminta's—the voice of one of Aminta's family. She had the trick of Aminta's upper lip in speaking. Her look on him was foreign; a civil smile as they conversed. She was very much at home with my lord, whom she rallied for his addiction to his Club at a particular hour of the afternoon. She conversed readily. She reminded him incidentally that her aunt would arrive early next day. He informed her, some time after, of an engagement " to tiffin with a brother officer," and she nodded.

They drove away together while the secretary was at his labour of sorting the heap of autobiographical scraps in a worn dispatch-box, pen and pencil jottings tossed to swell the mass when they had relieved an angry reminiscence. He noticed, heedlessly at the moment, feminine handwriting on some few clear sheets among them.

Next day he was alone in the library. He sat before the box, opened it and searched, merely to quiet his annoyance for having left those sheets of the fair amanuensis unexamined. They were not discoverable. They had gone.

He stood up at the stir of the door. It was she, and she acknowledged his bow; she took her steps to her chair.

He was informed that Lord Ormont had an engagement, and he remarked, "I can do the work very well." She sat quite silent.

He read first lines of the scraps, laid them in various places, as in a preparation for conjurer's tricks at cards; refraining from a glance, lest he should disconcert the eyes he felt to be on him fitfully.

At last she spoke, and he knew Aminta in his hearing and sight.

"Is Émile Grenat still anglomane?"

An instant before her voice was heard he had been persuading himself that the points of unlikeness between his young Aminta and this tall and stately lady of the proud reserve in her bearing flouted the resemblance.

CHAPTER V.

IN WHICH THE SHADES OF BROWNY AND MATEY ADVANCE AND RETIRE.

"Émile is as anglomane as ever, and not a bit less a Frenchman," Weyburn said, in a tone of one who muffles a shock at the heart.

"It would be the poorer compliment to us," she rejoined.

They looked at one another; she dropped her eyelids, he looked away.

She had the grand manner by nature. She was the woman of the girl once known.

"A soldier, is he?"

"Émile's profession and mine are much alike, or will be."

"A secretary?"

Her deadness of accent was not designed to carry her opinion of the post of secretary.

It brought the reply: "We hope to be schoolmasters."

She drew in a breath; there was a thin short voice, hardly voice, as when one of the unschooled minor feelings has been bruised. After a while she said—

"Does he think it a career?"

"Not brilliant."

"He was formed for a soldier."

"He had to go as the road led."

"A young man renouncing ambition!"

"Considering what we can do best."

"It signifies the taste for what he does."

"Certainly that."

Weyburn had senses to read the word "schoolmaster" in repetition behind her shut mouth. He was sharply sensible of a fall.

The task with his papers occupied him. If he had a wish, it was to sink so low in her esteem as to be spurned. A kick would have been a refreshment. Yet he was unashamed of the cause invoking it. We are instruments to the touch of certain women, and made to play strange tunes.

"Mr. Cuper flourishes?"

"The school exists. I have not been down there. I met Mr. Shalders yesterday. He has left the school."

"You come up from Olmer?"

"I was at Olmer last week, Lady Ormont."

An involuntary beam from her eyes thanked him for her title at that juncture of the dialogue. She grew more spirited.

"Mr. Shalders has joined the Dragoons, has he?"

"The worthy man has a happy imagination. He goes through a campaign daily."

"It seems to one to dignify his calling."

"I like his enthusiasm."

The lady withdrew into her thoughts; Weyburn fell upon his work.

* Mention of the military cloak of enthusiasm covering Shalders, brought the scarce credible old time to smite at his breast, in the presence of these eyes. A ringing of her title of Lady Ormont rendered the present time the incredible.

"I can hardly understand a young Frenchman's not entering the army," she said.

"The Napoleonic legend is weaker now," said he.

"The son of an officer!"

"Grandson."

"It was his choice to be,—he gave it up without reluctance?"

"Émile obeyed the command of his

parents," Weyburn answered; and he was obedient to the veiled direction of her remark, in speaking of himself: "I had a reason, too."

"One wonders!"

"It would have impoverished my mother's income to put aside a small allowance for me for years. She would not have hesitated. I then set my mind on the profession of schoolmaster."

"Émile Grenat was a brave boy. Has he no regrets?"

"Neither of us has a regret."

"He began ambitiously."

"It's the way at the beginning."

"It is not usually abjured."

"I'm afraid we neither of us 'dignify our calling' by discontent with it!"

A dusky flush, worth seeing, came on her cheeks. "I respect enthusiasms," she said, and it was as good to him to hear as the begging pardon, though clearly she could not understand enthusiasm for the schoolmaster's career.

Light of evidence was before him, that she had a friendly curiosity to know what things had led to their new meeting under these conditions. He sketched them cursorily; there was little to tell—little, that is, appealing to a romantic mind for interest. Aware of it, by sympathy, he degraded the narrative to a flatness about as cheering as a suburban London Sunday's promenade. Sympathy caused the perverseness. He felt her disillusionment, felt with it and spread a feast of it. She had to hear of studies at Caen and at a Paris Lycée; French fairly mastered; German, the same; Italian, the same; after studies at Heidelberg, Asti, and Florence; between four and five months at Athens (he was needlessly precise), in tutorship with a young nobleman: no events, nor a spot of colour. Thus did he wilfully, with pain to himself, put an extinguisher on the youth painted brilliant and eminent in a maiden's imagination.

"So there can no longer be thought of the army," she remarked; and the remark had a sort of sigh, though her breathing was equable.

"Unless a big war knocks over all rules and the country comes praying us to serve," he said.

"You would not refuse then?"

"Not in case of need. One may imagine a crisis when they would give commissions to men of my age or older for the cavalry— heavy losses of officers."

She spoke, as if urged by a sting to revert to the distasteful: "That profession—must you not take . . . enter into orders if you would . . . if you aim at any distinction?"

"And a member of the Anglican Church would not be allowed to exchange his frock for a cavalry sabre," said he. "That is true. I do not propose to settle as a schoolmaster in England."

"Where?"

"On the Continent."

"Would not America be better?"

"It would not so well suit the purpose in view for us."

"There are others besides?"

"Besides Émile, there is a German and an Italian and a Swiss."

"It is a Company?"

"A Company of schoolmasters! Companies of all kinds are forming. Colleges are Companies. And they have their collegians. Our aim is at pupils; we have no ambition for any title higher than School and Schoolmaster; it is not a Company."

So, like Nature parading her skeleton to youthful adorers of her face, he insisted on reducing to hideous material wreck the fair illusion, which had once arrayed him in alluring promise.

She explained: "I said, America. You would be among Protestants in America."

"Catholics and Protestants are both welcome to us, according to our scheme. And Germans, French, English, Americans, Italians, if they will come; Spaniards and Portuguese, and Scandinavians, Russians as well. And Jews; Mahommedans too, if only they will come! The more mixed, the more it hits our object."

"You have not stated where on the Continent it is to be."

"The spot fixed on is in Switzerland."

"You will have scenery."

"I hold to that, as an influence."

A cool vision of the Bernese Alps encircled the young schoolmaster; and she said, "It would influence girls, I dare say."

"A harder matter with boys, of course— at first. We think we may make it serve."

"And where is the spot? Is that fixed on?"

"Fifteen miles from Berne, on elevated land, neighbouring a water, not quite to be called a lake, unless in an auctioneer's advertisement."

"I am glad of the lake. I could not look on a country home where there was no swimming. You will be head of the school."

"There must be a head."

"Is the school likely to be established soon?"

He fell into her dead tone: "Money is required for establishments. I have a Reversion coming some day; I don't dabble in *post obits*."

He waited for further questions. They were at an end.

"You have your work to do, Mr. Weyburn."

Saying that, she bowed an implied apology

for having kept him from it, and rose. She bowed again as she passed through the doorway, in acknowledgment of his politeness.

Here, then, was the end of the story of Browny and Matey. Such was his thought under the truncheon-stroke of their colloquy. Lines of Browny's letters were fiery waving ribands about him, while the coldly gracious bow of the lady wrote Finis.

The gulf between the two writings remained unsounded. It gave a heave to the old passion, but stirred no new one; he had himself in hand now, and he shut himself up when the questions bred of amazement buzzed and threatened to storm. After all, what is not curious in this world? The curious thing would be if curious things should fail to happen. Men have been saying it since they began to count and turn corners. And let us hold off from speculating when there is or but seems a shadow of unholiness over that mole-like business. There shall be no questions; and as to feelings, the same. They, if petted for a moment beneath the shadow, corrupt our blood. Weyburn was a man to have them by the throat at the birth.

Still they thronged; heavy work of strangling had to be done. Her tone of disappointment with the schoolmaster bit him, and it flattered him. The feelings leapt alive, equally venomous from the wound and the caress. They pushed to see, had to be repelled from seeing, the girl Browny in the splendid woman; they had lightning memories: not the pain of his grip could check their voice on the theme touching her happiness or the reverse. And this was an infernal cunning. He paused perforce to inquire, giving them space for the breeding of their multitudes. Was she happy? Did she not seem too meditative, enclosed, toneless, at her age? Vainly the persecuted fellow said to himself: "But what is it to me now?"—The Browny days were over. The passion for the younger Aminta was over—buried; and a dream of power belonging to those days was not yet more than visionary. It had moved her once, when it was a young soldier's. She treated the schoolmaster's dream as vapour, and the old days as dead and ghostless. She did rightly. How could they or she or he be other than they were!

With that sage exclamation, he headed into the Browny days and breasted them; and he had about him the living foamy sparkle of the very time, until the Countess of Ormont breathed the word "Schoolmaster"; when, at once, it was dusty land where buoyant waters had been, and the armies of the facts, in uniform drab, with some feathers and laces, and a significant surpliced figure, decorously covering the wildest of Cupids, marched the standard of the winking gold-piece, which is their nourishing sun and eclipser of all suns that foster dreams.

As you perceive, he was drawing swiftly to the vortex of the fools, and round and round he went, lucky to float.

His view of the business of the schoolmaster plucked him from the whirl. She despised it; he upheld it. He stuck to his view, finding their antagonism on the subject wholesome for him. All that she succeeded in doing was to rob it of the aurora colour clothing everything on which Matey Weyburn set his aim. Her contempt of it, whether as a profession in itself or as one suitable to the former young enthusiast for arms, dwarfed it to appear like the starved plants under Greenland skies. But those are of a sturdy genus; they mean to live; they live, perforce, of the right to live; they will prove their right in a coming season, when some one steps near and wonders at them, and from more closely observing, gets to understand, learning that the significance and the charm of earth will be as well shown by them as by her tropical fair flaunters or the tenderly-nurtured exotics.

An unopened coffer of things to be said in defence of—no, on behalf of—no, in honour of the Profession of Schoolmaster, perhaps to the convincing of Aminta, Lady Ormont, was glanced at; a sentence or two leapt out and stepped forward, and had to retire. He preferred to the fathering of tricky, windy phrases, the being undervalued—even by her. He was taught to see again how Rhetoric haunts, and Rhetoric bedevils, the vindication of the clouded, especially in the case of a disesteemed Profession requiring one to raise it and impose it upon the antagonistic senses for the bewildering of the mind. One has to sound it loudly; there is no treating it, as in the advocacy of the cases of flesh and blood, with the masterly pathos of designed simplicity. And Weyburn was Cuper's Matey Weyburn still in his loathing of artifice to raise emotion, loathing of the affected, the stilted, the trumpet of speech —always excepting school-exercises in the tongues, the unmasking of a Catiline, the address of a general, Athenian or other, to troops.

He kept his coffer shut; and, for a consequence, he saw the contents as an avenue of blossom leading to vistas of infinite harvest.

She was Lady Ormont: Aminta shared the title of his old hero! He refused to speculate upon how it had come to pass, and let the curtain hang, though dramas and romances, with the miracles involved in them, were agitated by a transient glimpse at the curtain.

Well! and he hoped to be a member of

the Profession she despised : hoped it with all his heart. And one good effect of his giving his heart to the hope was, that he could hold from speculating and from feeling, even from pausing to wonder at the most wonderful turn of events. Blessed antagonism drove him to be braced by thoughts upon the hardest of the schoolmaster's tasks —bright winter thoughts, prescribing to him satisfaction with a faith in the sowing, which may be his only reaping. Away fly the boys in sheaves. After his toil with them, to instruct, restrain, animate, point their minds, they leave him, they plunge into the world and are gone. Will he see them again ? It is a flickering perhaps. To sustain his belief that he has done serviceable work, he must be sure of his having charged them with good matter. How can the man do it, if, during his term of apprenticeship, he has allowed himself to dally here and there, down to moony dreamings over inscrutable beautiful eyes of a married lady;. for the sole reason that he meets her unexpectedly, after an exchange of letters with her in long-past days at school, when she was an inexperienced girl, who knew not what she vowed, and he a flighty-headed youngster, crying out to be the arrow of any bow that was handy? Yes, she was once that girl, named Browny by the boys.

Temptation threw warm light on the memory, and very artfully, by conjuring up the faces, cries, characters, all the fun of the boys. There was no possibility of forgetting her image in those days; he had, therefore, to live with it and to live near the grown woman—Time's present answer to the old riddle. It seemed to him that, instead of sorting ⸺Lord Ormont's papers, he ought to be at sharp exercise. According to his prescript, sharp exercise of lungs and limbs is a man's moral aid against temptation. He knew it as the one trusty antidote for him, who was otherwise the vessel of a temperament pushing to mutiny. Certainly it is the best philosophy youth can pretend to practise; and Lord Ormont kept him from it! Worse than that, the slips and sheets of paper in the dispatch-box were not an exercise of the mind even; there was nothing to grapple with — no diversion; criticism passed by them indulgently, if not benevolently.

Quite apart from the subject inscribed on them, Weyburn had now and again a blow at the breast, of untraceable origin. For he was well enough aware that the old days when Browny imagined him a hero, in drinking his praises of a brighter, were drowned. They were dead; but here was she the bride of the proved hero. His praises might have helped in causing her willingness —devotional readiness—he could fancy— to yield her hand. Perhaps at the moment when the hero was penning some of the Indian slips here, the boy at school was preparing Aminta; but he could not be responsible for a sacrifice of the kind suggested by Lady Charlotte. And no, there had been no such sacrifice, although Lord Ormont's inexplicable treatment of his young countess, under cover of his notorious reputation with women, conduced to the suspicion.

While the vagrant in Weyburn was thus engaged, his criticism of the soldier-lord's field-English on paper let the stuff go tolerantly unexamined, but with a degree of literary contempt at heart for the writer who had that woman-scented reputation and expressed himself so poorly. The sentiment was outside of reason. We do, nevertheless, expect our Don Juans to deliver their minds a trifle elegantly, if not in classic English, on paper; and when we find one of them inflicting cruelty, as it appears, and the victim is a young woman, a beautiful young woman, she pleads to us poetically against the bearish sentences of his composition. We acknowledge, however, that a mere sentiment, entertained possibly by us alone, should not be permitted to condemn him unheard.

Lady Ormont was not seen again. After luncheon at a solitary table, the secretary worked till winter's lamps were lit; and then shone freedom, with assurance to him that he would escape from the miry mental ditch he had been floundering in since Aminta revealed herself. Sunday was the glorious day to follow, with a cleansing bath of a walk along the southern hills; homely English scenery to show to a German friend, one of his "Company." Half-a-dozen good lads were pledged to the walk; bearing which in view, it could be felt that this nonsensical puzzlement over his relations to the moods and tenses of a married woman would be bounced out of recollection before nightfall. The landscape given off any of the airy hills of Surrey would suffice to do it.

A lady stood among her boxes below, as he descended the stairs to cross the hall. He knew her for the person Lady Charlotte called "the woman's aunt," whom Lord Ormont could not endure—a forgiven old enemy, Mrs. Nargett Pagnell.

He saluted. She stared, and corrected her incivility with "Ah, yes," and a formal smile.

If not accidentally delayed on her journey, she had been needlessly the cause why Lord Ormont hugged his Club during the morning and afternoon. Weyburn was pushed to think of the matter by remembrance of his foregone resentment at her having withdrawn Aminta from Miss Vincent's three days earlier than the holiday time. The resentment was over; but a germ of it must have sprung from the dust to prompt the kindling leap his memory took, out of all due connection, like a lightning among the crags. It struck Aminta smartly. He called to mind the conversation at table yesterday. Had she played on Lord Ormont's dislike of the aunt to drive him forth for some purpose of her own? If so, the little trick had been done with deplorable spontaneity or adeptness of usage. What was the purpose?—to converse with an old acquaintance, undisturbed by Lord Ormont and her aunt? Neatly done, supposing the surmise correct.

But what was there in the purpose? He sifted rapidly for the gist of the conversation; reviewed the manner of it, the words, the sound they had, the feelings they touched; then owned that the question could not be answered. Owning, further, that the recurrence of these idiotic speculations, feelings, questions, wrote him down as both dull fellow and impertinent, he was enabled to restore Aminta to the queenly place she took above the schoolmaster, who was very soon laughing at his fever or flush of the afternoon. The day had brought a great surprise, nothing more. Twenty minutes of fencing in the *salle d'armes* of an Italian captain braced him to health, and shifted scenes of other loves, lighter loves, following the Browny days— not to be called loves; in fact, hardly beyond inclinations. Nevertheless, inclinations are an infidelity. To meet a married woman, and be mooning over her because she gave him her eyes and her handwriting when a girl, was enough to rouse an honest fellow's laugh at himself, in the contemplation of his intermediate amorous vagabondage. Had he ever known the veritable passion after Browny sank from his ken? Let it be confessed, never His first love was his only true love, despite one shuddering episode, oddly humiliating to recollect, though he had not behaved badly. So, then, by right of his passion, thus did eternal justice rule it: that Browny belonged to Matey Weyburn, Aminta to Lord Ormont. Aminta was a lady blooming in the flesh, Browny was the past's pale phantom; for which reason he could call her his own, without harm done to any one, and with his usual appetite for, dinner, breakfast, lunch, whatever the meal supplied by the hour.

It would somewhat alarmingly have got to Mr. Weyburn's conscience through a disturbance of his balance, telling him that he was on a perilous road, if his relish for food had been blunted. He had his axiom on the subject, and he was wrong in the general instances, for the appetites of rogues and ogres are not known to fail. As regarded himself, he was eminently right; and he could apply it to boys also, to all young people—the unlaunched, he called them. He counted himself among the launched, no doubt, and had breasted seas; but the boy was alive, a trencherman lad, in the coming schoolmaster, and told him profitable facts concerning his condition, besides throwing a luminous ray on the arcana of our elusive youthful. If they have no stout zest for eating, put QUERY against them.

His customary enjoyment of dinner convinced Mr. Weyburn that he had not brooded morbidly over his phantom Browny, and could meet Aminta, Countess of Ormont, on the next occasion with the sentiments proper to a common official. Did she not set him a commendable example? He admired her for not concealing her disdain of the aspirant schoolmaster, quite comprehending, by sympathy, why the woman should reproach the girl who had worshipped heroes, if this was a full-grown specimen; and the reply of the shamed girl that, in her ingorance, she could not know better. He spared the girl, but he laughed at the woman he commended, laughed at himself.

Aminta's humour was being stirred about the same time. She and her aunt were at the dinner-table in the absence of my lord. The dinner had passed with the stiff dialogue peculiar to couples under supervision of their inferiors; and, as soon as the room was clear, she had asked her aunt, touching the secretary: "Have you seen him?"

Mrs. Nargett Pagnell's answer could have been amusing only to one whose intimate knowledge of her found it characteristically salt; for she was a lady of speech addressed ever directly or roundabout to the chief point of business between herself and her hearer, and the more she was brief, oblique, far-shooting, the more comically intelligible she was to her niece. She bent her head to signify that she had seen the secretary, and struck the table with both hands, exclaiming:

"Well, to be sure, Lord Ormont!"

Their discussion, before they descended the stairs to dinner, concerned his lordship's extraordinary indifference to the thronging of handsome young men around his young countess.

Here, the implication ran, is one established in the house.

Aminta's thoughts could be phrased: "Yes, that is true, for one part of it."

As for the other part, the ascent of a Phœbus Apollo, with his golden bow and quiver of the fairest of Eastern horizon skies, followed suddenly by the sight of him toppling over in Mr. Cuper's long-skirted brown coat, with spectacles and cane, is an image that hardly exceeds the degradation she conceived. It was past ludicrous; yet admitted of no woefulness, nothing soothingly pathetic. It smothered and barked at the dreams of her blooming spring of life, to which her mind had latterly been turning back, for an escape from sour, one may say cynical, reflections, the present issue of a beautiful young woman's first savour of battle with the world.

CHAPTER VI.

IN A MOOD OF LANGUOR.

UP in Aminta's amber dressing-room, Mrs. Nargett Pagnell alluded sadly to the long month of separation, and begged her niece to let her have in plain words an exact statement of the present situation; adding, "Items will do." Thereupon she slipped into prattle and held the field.

She was the known, worthy, good, intolerable woman whom the burgess turns out for his world in regiments, that do and look and all but step alike; and they mean well, and have conventional worships and material aspirations, and very peculiar occult refinements, with a blind head and a haphazard gleam of acuteness, impressive to acquaintances, convincing themselves that they impersonate sagacity. She had said this, done that; and it was, by proof, Providence consenting, the right thing. A niece, written down in her girlhood, because of her eyes and her striking air and excellent deportment, as mate for a nobleman, marries him before she is out of her teens. "I said, She shall be a countess." A countess she is. Providence does not comply with our predictions in order to stultify us. Admitting the position of affairs for the moment as extraordinary, we are bound by what has happened to expect they will be conformable in the end. Temporarily warped, we should say of them.

She could point to the reason: it was Lord Ormont's blunt misunderstanding of her character. The burgess's daughter was refining to an appreciation of the exquisite so rapidly that she could criticize patricians.

My lord had never forgiven her for correcting him in his pronunciation of her name by marriage. Singular indeed; but men, even great men, men of title, are so, some of them, whom you could least suspect of their being so. He would speak the "g" in Nargett, and he declined—after a remonstrance he declined—to pass Pagnell under the cedilla. Lord Ormont spoke the name like a man hating it, or an English rustic: "Nargett Pagnell," instead of the soft and elegant "Naryett Pagñell," the only true way of speaking it; and she had always taken that pronunciation of her name for a test of people's breeding. The expression of his lordship's countenance under correction was memorable. Naturally, in those honeymoony days, the young Countess of Ormont sided with her husband the earl; she declared that her aunt had never dreamed of the cedilla before the expedition to Spain. When, for example, Alfred

Nargett Pagnell had a laughing remark, which Aminta in her childhood must have heard: "We rhyme with spaniel!"

That was the secret of Lord Ormont's prepossession against Aminta's aunt; and who can tell? perhaps of much of his behaviour to the beautiful young wife he at least admired, sincerely admired, though he caused her to hang her head—cast a cloud on the head so dear to him!

Otherwise there was no interpreting his lordship. To think of herself as personally disliked by a nobleman stupefied Mrs. Pagnell, from her just expectation of reciprocal dealings in high society; for she confessed herself a fly to a title. Where is the shame, if titles are created to attract? Elsewhere than in that upper circle, we may anticipate hard bargains; the widow of a solicitor had not to learn it. But when a distinguished member and ornament of the chosen seats above blew cold upon their gesticulatory devotee, and was besides ungrateful, she was more than commonly assured of his being, as she called him, " a sphinx." His behaviour to his legally-wedded wife confirmed the charge.

She checked her flow to resume the question. " So, then, where are we now? He allows you liberally for pin-money in addition to your own small independent income. Satisfaction with that would warrant him to suppose his whole duty done by you."

" We are where we were, aunty; the month has made no change," said Aminta, in languor.

" And you as patient as ever?"

" I am supposed to have everything a woman can require."

" Can he possibly think it? And I have to warn you, child, that lawyers are not so absolving as the world is with some of the ladies Lord Ormont allows you to call your friends. I have been hearing—it is not mere airy tales one hears from lawyers about cases in Courts of Law. Tighten your lips as you like; I say nothing to condemn or reflect on Mrs. Lawrence Finchley. I have had my eyes a little opened, that is all. Oh, I know my niece Aminta, when it's a friend to stand by; but our position—thanks to your inscrutable lord and master—demands of us the utmost scrupulousness, or it soon becomes a whirl and scandal flying about, and those lawyers picking up and putting together. I have had a difficulty to persuade them! . . . and my own niece! whom I saw married at the British Embassy in Madrid, as I take good care to tell everybody; for it was my doing; I am the responsible person! and by an English Protestant clergyman, to all appearance able to walk erect in and out of any of these excellent new Life Assurance offices they are starting for the benefit of widows and orphans, and deceased within six days of the ceremony—if ceremony one may call the hasty affair in those foreign places. My dear, the instant I heard it I had a presentiment, 'All has gone well up to now.' I remember murmuring the words. Then your letter, received in that smelly Barcelona: Lord Ormont was carrying you off to Granada—a dream of my infancy! It may not have been his manœuvre, but it was the beginning of his manœuvres."

Aminta shuddered. "And tra-la-la, and castañets, and my Cid! my Cid! and the Alhambra, the Sierra Nevada, and ay di me, Alhama; and Boabdil el Chico and el Zagal and Fray Antonio Agapida!" She flung out the rattle, yawning, with her arms up and her head back, in the posture of a woman wounded. One of her aunt's chance shots had traversed her breast, flashing at her the time, the scene, the husband, intensest sunniness on sword-edges of shade,—and now the wedded riddle, illusion dropping mask, romance in its anatomy, cold English mist. Ah, what a background is the present when we have the past to the fore! That filmy past is diaphanous on heaving ribs.

She smiled at the wide-eyed little gossip. "Don't speak of manœuvres, dear aunt. And we'll leave Granada to the poets. I'm tired. Talk of our own people, on your side and my father's, and as much as you please of the Pagnell-Pagñells, they refresh me. Do they go on marrying?"

"Why, my child, how could they go on without it?"

Aminta pressed her hands at her eyelids. "Oh, me!" she sighed, feeling the tear come with a sting from checked laughter. "But there are marriages, aunty, that don't go on, though Protestant clergymen officiated. Leave them unnoticed, I have really nothing to tell."

"You have not heard anything of Lady Eglett?"

"Lady Charlotte Eglett? No syllable. Or wait—my lord's secretary was with her at Olmer; approved by her, I have to suppose."

"There, my dear, I say again I do dread that woman, if she can make a man like Lord Ormont afraid of her. And no doubt she is of our old aristocracy. And they tell me she is coarse in her conversation—like a man. Lawyers tell me she is never happy but in litigation. Years back, I am given to understand, she did not set so particularly good an example. Lawyers hear next to everything. I am told she lifted her horsewhip on a gentleman once, and then put her horse at him and rode him down. You will say, the sister of your husband. No; not to make my niece a countess, would I, if I had known the kind of family! Then one asks, Is she half as much afraid of him? In that case, no wonder they have given up meeting. Was formerly one of the Keepsake Beauties. Well, Lady Eglett, and Aminta, Countess of Ormont, will be in that Peerage, as they call it, let her only have her dues. My dear, I would—if I ever did—swear the woman is jealous."

"Of me, aunty!"

"I say more; I say again, it would be a good thing for somebody if somebody had his twitch of jealousy. Wives may be too meek. Cases and cases my poor Alfred read to me, where an ill-behaving man was brought to his senses by a clever little shuffle of the cards, and by the most innocent of wives. A kind of poison to him, of course; but there are poisons that cure. It might come into the courts; and the nearer the proofs the happier he in withdrawing from his charge and effecting a reconciliation. Short of guilt, of course.

Men are so strange. Imagine now, if a handsome young woman were known to be admired rather more than enough by a good-looking gentleman near about her own age. Oh, I've no patience with the man for causing us to think and scheme! Only there are men who won't be set right unless we do. My husband used to say, change is such a capital thing in life's jog-trot, that men find it refreshing if we now and then reverse the order of our pillion-riding for them. A spiritless woman in a wife is what they bear least of all. Anything rather. Is Mr. Morsfield haunting Mrs. Lawrence Finchley's house as usual?"

Aminta's cheeks unrolled their deep damask rose at the abrupt intrusion of the name. "I meet him there."

"Lord Adderwood, Sir John Randeller, and the rest?"

"Two or three times a week."

"And the lady, wife of the captain,

really a Lady Fair—Mrs. . . . month of May; so I have to get at it."

"She may be seen there."

"Really a contrast, when you two are together! As to reputation, there is an exchange of colours. Those lawyers hold the keys of the great world, and a naughty world it is, I fear—with exceptions, who are the salt, but don't taste so much. I can't help enjoying the people at Mrs. Lawrence Finchley's. I like to feel I can amuse them, as they do me. One puzzles for what they say—in somebody's absence, I mean. They must take Lord Ormont for a perfect sphinx; unless they are so silly as to think they may despise him, or suppose him indifferent. Oh, that upper class! It's a garden, and we can't help pushing to enter it; and fair flowers, indeed, but serpents too, like the tropics. It tries us more than anything else in the world—well, just as good eating tries the constitution.

He ought to know it and feel it, and give his wife all the protection of his name, instead of—not that he denies: I have brought him to that point; he cannot deny it with me. But not to present her—to shun the Court; not to introduce her to his family, to appear ashamed of her! My darling Aminta, a month of absence for reflection on your legally-wedded husband's conduct increases my astonishment. For usually men old enough to be the grandfathers of their wives——"

"Oh, pray, aunty, pray, pray!" Aminta cried, and her body writhed. "No more to-night. You mean well, I am sure. Let us wait. I shall sleep, perhaps, if I go to bed early. I dare say I am spiritless—not worth more than I get. I gave him the lead altogether; he keeps it. In everything else he is kind; I have all the luxuries—enough to loathe them. Kiss me and say good-night."

Aminta made it imperative by rising. Her aunt stood up, kissed, and exclaimed, "I tell you you are a queenly creature, not to be treated as any puny trollop of a handmaid. And although he is a great nobleman, he is not to presume to behave any longer, my dear, as if your family had no claim on his consideration. My husband, Alfred Pagnell, would have laid that before him pretty quick. You are the child of the Farrells and the Solers, both old families; on your father's side you are linked with the oldest nobility in Europe. It flushes one to think of it! Your grandmother, marrying Captain Algernon Farrell, was the legitimate daughter of a Grandee of Spain, as I have told Lord Ormont often, and I defy him to equal that for a romantic marriage in the annals of his house, or boast of bluer blood. Again, the Solers——"

"We take the Solers for granted, aunty: good-night."

"Commoners, if you like; but established since the Conquest. That is, we trace the pedigree. And to be treated, even by a great nobleman, as if we were stuff picked up out of the ditch! I declare, there are times when I sit and think and boil. Is it chivalrous, is it generous—is it, I say, decent — is it what Alfred would have called a fair fulfilment of a pact, for your wedded husband—? You may close my mouth! But he pretends to be chivalrous and generous, and he has won a queen any wealthy gentleman in England — I know of one, if not two—would be proud to have beside him in equal state; and what is he to her? He is an extinguisher. Or is it the very meanest miserliness, that he may keep you all to himself? There we are again! I say he is an unreadable sphinx."

Aminta had rung the bell for her maid. Mrs. Pagnell could be counted on for drawing in her tongue when the domestics were near.

A languor past delivery in sighs was on the young woman's breast. She could have heard without a regret that the heart was to cease beating. Had it been downright misery she would have looked about her with less of her exanimate glassiness. The unhappy have a form of life: until they are worn out, they feel keenly. She felt nothing. The blow to her pride of station and womanhood struck on numbed sensations. She could complain that the blow was not heavier.

A letter lying in her jewel-box called her to read it, for the chance of some slight stir. The contents were known. The signature of Adolphus Morsfield had a new meaning for her eyes, and dashed her at her husband in a spasm of revolt and wrath against the man exposing her to these letters, which a motion of her hand could turn to blood, and abstention from any sign maintained in a Satanic whisper, saying, "Here lies one way of solving the riddle." It was her husband who drove her to look that way.

The look was transient, and the wrath: she could not burn. A small portion of contempt lodged in her mind to shadow husbands precipitating women on their armoury for a taste of vengeance. Women can always be revenged—so speedily, so completely: they have but to dip. Husbands driving wives to taste their power execrate the creature for her fall deep downward. They are forgetful of causes.

Does it matter? Aminta's languor asked. The letter had not won a reply. Thought of the briefest of replies was a mountain of effort, and she moaned at her nervelessness in body and mind. To reply, to reproach the man, to be flame—an image of herself under the form she desired—gave her a momentary false energy, wherein the daring of the man, whose life was at a toss for the writing of this letter, hung lighted. She had therewith a sharp vision of his features, repellent in correctness, Greek in lines, with close eyes, hollow temples, pressed lips—a face indicating the man who can fling himself on a die. She had heard tales of women and the man. Some had loved him, report said. Here were words to say that he loved her. They might, poor man, be true. Otherwise she had never been loved.

Memory had of late been paying visits to a droopy plant in the golden summer drought on a gorgeous mid-sea island, and had taken her on board to refresh her with voyages, always bearing down full sail on a couple of blissful schools, abodes of bloom and briny vigour, sweet merriment, innocent longings, dreams the shyest, dreams the mightiest. At night before sleep, at morn before rising, often during day, and when vexed or when dispirited, she had issued her command for the voyage. Sheer refreshment followed, as is ever the case if our vessel carries no freight of hopes. There could be no hopes. It was forgotten that they had ever been seriously alive. But it carried an admiration. Now, an admiration may endure, and this one had been justified all round. The figure heroical, the splendid, active youth, hallowed Aminta's past. The past of a bitterly humiliated Aminta was a garden in the coming kiss of sunset, with that godlike figure of young manhood to hallow it. There he stayed, perpetually assuring her of his triumphs to come.

She could have no further voyages. Ridicule convulsed her home of refuge. For the young soldier-hero to be unhorsed by misfortune, was one thing; but the meanness of the ambition he had taken in exchange for the thirst of glory, accused his nature. He so certainly involved her in the burlesque of the transformation that she had to quench memory.

She was, therefore, having smothered a good part of herself, accountably languid —a condition alternating with fire in Aminta; and as Mr. Morsfield's letter supplied the absent element, her needy instinct pushed her to read his letter through. She had not yet done that with attention.

Whether a woman loves a man or not, he is her lover if he dare tell her he loves her, and is heard with attention. Aware that the sentences were poison, she summoned her constitutional antagonism to the mad step proposed, so far nullifying the virus as to make her shrink from the madness. Even then her soul cried out to her husband, Who drives me to read? or rather, to brood upon what she read. The brooding ensued, was the thirst of her malady.

The best antidote she could hit on was the writer's face. Yet it expressed him, his fire and his courage—gifts she respected in him, found wanting in herself. Read by Lord Ormont, this letter would mean a deadly thing.

Aminta did her lord the justice to feel sure of him, that with her name bearing the superscription, it might be left on her table, and would not have him to peruse it. If he manœuvred, it was never basely. Despite resentment, her deepest heart denied his being indifferent either to her honour or his own in relation to it. He would vindicate both at a stroke, for a sign. Nevertheless, he had been behaving cruelly. She charged on him the guilt of the small preludes, archeries, anglings, veilings, evasions, all done with the eyelids and the mute of the lips, or a skirmisher word or a fan's flourish, and which, intended to pique the husband rather than incite the lover, had led Mrs. Lawrence Finchley to murmur at her ear, in close assembly, without a distinct designation of Mr. Morsfield, "Dangerous man to play little games with!" It had brought upon her this letter of declaration, proposal, entreaty.

This letter was the man's life in her hands, and safe, of course. But surely it was a proof that the man loved her?

Aminta was in her five-and-twentieth year; when the woman who is uncertain of the having been loved, and she reputed beautiful, desirable, is impelled by a sombre necessity to muse on a declaration, and nibble at an idea of a test. If "a dangerous man to play little games with," he could scarcely be dangerous to a woman having no love for him at all. It meant merely that he would soon fall to writing letters like this, and he could not expect an answer to it. But her heart really thanked him, and wished the poor gentleman to take its dumb response as his reward, for being the one sole one who had loved her.

Aminta dwelt on "the one sole one." Lord Ormont's treatment had detached her from any belief in love on his part; and the schoolboy, now ambitious to become a schoolmaster, was behind the screen unlikely to be lifted again by a woman valuing her pride of youth, though he had —behold our deceptions!—the sympathetic face entirely absent from that of Mr. Adolphus Morsfield, whom the world would count quite as handsome—nay, it boasted him. He enjoyed the reputation of a killer of ladies. Women have odd tastes, Aminta thought, and examined the gentleman's handwriting. It pleased her better. She studied it till the conventional phrases took a fiery hue, and came at her with an invasive rush.

The letter was cast back into the box,

locked up; there an end to it, or no interdiction of sleep.

Sleep was a triumph. Aminta's healthy frame rode her over petty agitations of a blood uninflamed, as lightly as she swam the troubled sea-waters her body gloried to cleave. She woke in the morning peaceful and mildly reflective, like one who walks across green meadows. Only by degrees, by glimpses, was she drawn to remember the trotting, cantering, galloping, leaping of an active heart during night. We cannot, man or woman, control the heart in sleep at night. There had been wild leapings. Night will lead an unsatisfied heart of a woman, by way of sleep, to scale black mountains, jump jagged chasms. Sleep is a horse that laughs at precipices and abysses. We bid women, moreover, be all heart. They are to cultivate their hearts, pay much heed to their hearts. The vast realm of feeling is open to these appointed keepers of the sanctuary household, who may be withering virgins, may be childless matrons, may be unhusbanded wives. Wandering in the vast realm which they are exhorted to call their own, for the additional attractiveness it gives them, an unsatisfied heart of woman will somewhat audaciously cross the borderland a single step into the public road of the vast realm of thinking. Once there, and but a single step on the road, she is a rebel against man's law for her sex. Nor is it urgent on her that she should think defiantly in order to feel herself the rebel. She may think submissively, with a heart (the enlarged, the scientifically plumped, the pasture of epicurean man), with her coveted heart in revolt, and from the mere act of thinking at all.

Aminta reviewed perforce, dead against her will, certain of the near-to-happiness racings over-night. She thinned her lips, and her cheeks glowed. An arm, on the plea of rescuing, had been round her. The choice now offered her was, to yield to softness or to think. She took the latter step, the single step of an unaccustomed foot, which women educated simply to feel, will, upon extreme impulsion, take; and it held a candle in a windy darkness. She saw no Justice there. The sensational immensity touched sublime, short of that spirit of Justice required for the true sublime. And void of Justice, what a sunless place is any realm! Infants, the male and the female alike, first begin to know they feel when it is refused them. When they know they feel, they have begun to reflect. The void of Justice is a godless region. Women, to whom the solitary thought has come as a blown candle, illumining the fringes of their storm, ask themselves whether they are

God's creatures or man's. The question deals a sword-stroke of division between them and their human masters. Young women, animated by the passions their feeling bosoms of necessity breed, and under terror discover, do not distinguish an abstract justice from a concrete. They are of the tribe too long hereditarily enslaved to conceive an abstract. So it is with them, that their God is the God of the slave, as it is with all but the bravest of boys. He is a Thing to cry to, a Punisher, not much of a Supporter—the Biblical Hebrew's right reading of Nature, favouring man, yet prompt to confound him, and with woman for the instrument of vengeance. By such a maze the blindfolded are brought round to see Justice on earth. If women can only believe in some soul of justice, they will feel they belong to God—of the two; and the peril for them then is, that they will set the one incomprehensible Power in opposition to the other, urging their unsatisfied natures to make secret appeal away from man and his laws altogether, at the cost of losing clear sight of the God who shines in thought. It is a manner whereby the desperately harried among these creatures of the petted heart arrive upon occasion at an agreeable, almost reposeful, contemplation of the reverse of God.

There is little pleasure to be on the lecture-rostrum for a narrator sensible to the pulses of his audience. Justice compels at times. In truth, there are times when the foggy obscurities of the preacher are by comparison broad daylight beside the whirling loose tissues of a woman unexplained. Aminta was one born to prize rectitude, to walk on the traced line uprightly; and while the dark rose overflowed the soft brown of her cheeks, under musings upon her unlicenced heart's doings over-night, she not only pleaded for woeful creatures of her sex burdened as she and erring, she weighed them in the scales with men, and put her heart where Justice pointed, sending men to kick aloft.

Her husband, the man-riddle: she was unable to rede or read him. Her will could not turn him, nor her tongue combat; nor was it granted her to pique the mailed veteran. Every poor innocent little bit of an art had been exhausted. Her title was Lady Ormont: her condition actually slave. A luxuriously established slave, consorting with a singularly enfranchised set,—as, for instance, Mrs. Lawrence Finchley and Lord Adderwood; Sir John Randeller and Lady Staines; Mrs. May, Amy May, notorious wife of a fighting captain, the loveliest of blondes; and other ladies, other gentlemen,

Mr. Morsfield in the list, paired or not yet paired: gossip raged. Aminta was of a disposition too generously cordial to let her be the rigorous critic of people with whom she was in touch. But her mind knew relief when she recollected that her humble little school-mate, Selina Collett, who had suffered on her behalf in old days, was coming up to her from the Suffolk coast on a visit for a week. However much a slave and an unloved woman, she could be a constant and protecting friend. Besides, Lord Ormont was gracious to little Selina. She thought of his remarks about the modest-minded girl after first seeing her. From that she struck upon a notion of reserves of humaneness being in him, if she might find the path to them: and thence, fortified by the repose her picture of little Selina's merit had bestowed, she sprang to the idea of valiancy, that she would woo him to listen to her, without inflicting a scene. · He had been a listening lover, seeming lover, once, later than the Granada sunsets. The letter in her jewel-box urged Aminta to clear her conscience by some means, for leaving it unburnt.

CHAPTER VII.

EXHIBITS EFFECTS OF A PRATTLER'S DOSES.

The rules in Lord Ormont's household assisted to shelter him for some hours of the day from the lady who was like a blast of sirocco under his roof. He had his breakfast alone, as Lady Charlotte had it at Olmer; a dislike of a common table in the morning was a family trait with both. At ten o'clock the secretary arrived, and they were shut up together. At the luncheon table Aminta usually presided. If my lord dined at home, he had by that time established an equanimity rendering his constant civility to Mrs. Pagnell less arduous. The presence of a woman of tongue, perpetually on the spring to gratify him and win him, was among the burdens he bore for his Aminta.

Mrs. Pagnell soon perceived that the secretary was in favour. My lord and this Mr. Weyburn had their pet themes of conversation, upon which the wary aunt of her niece did not gaze like the wintry sun with the distant smile her niece displayed over discussions concerning military biographies, Hannibal's use of his elephants and his Numidian horse, the Little St. Bernard, modern artillery, ancient slingers, English and Genoese bowmen, Napoleon's tactics, his command to the troopers to "give point," and English officers' neglect of sword exercise, and the "devil of a day" Old England is to have on a day to come. My lord connected our day of trial with India. Mrs. Pagnell assumed an air of studious interest; she struck in to give her niece a lead, that Lord Ormont might know his countess capable of joining the driest of subjects occupying exalted minds. Aminta did not follow her; and she was extricated gallantly by the gentlemen in turn.

The secretary behaved with a pretty civility. Aminta shook herself to think tolerantly of him when he, after listening to the suggestion, put interrogatively, that we should profit by Hannibal's example and train elephants to serve as a special army corps for the perfect security of our priceless Indian Empire, instanced the danger likely to result from their panic fear of cannon, and forbore to consult Lord Ormont's eye.

Mrs. Pagnell knew that she had put her foot into it; but women advised of being fools in what they say, are generally sustained by their sense of the excellent motive which impelled them. Even to the Countess of Ormont, she could have replied, "We might have given them a higher idea of us"—if, that meant, the Countess of

Ormont had entered the field beside her, to the exclusion of a shrinking Aminta. She hinted as much subsequently, and Aminta's consciousness of the truth was touched. The young schoolmaster's company sat on her spirits, deadened her vocabulary. Her aunt spoke of passing the library door and hearing the two gentlemen loudly laughing. It seemed subserviency on the fallen young hero's part. His tastes were low. He frequented the haunts of boxing men; her lord informed her of his having made, or of his making, matches to run or swim or walk certain distances against competitors or within a given time. He had also half-a-dozen boys or more in tow, whom he raced out of town on Sundays; a nucleus of the school he intended to form.

But will not Achilles become by comparison a common rushlight where was a blazing torch, if we see him clap a clown's cap on the head whose golden helm was fired by Pallas?

Nay, and let him look the hero still: all the more does he point finger on his meanness of nature.

Turning to another, it is another kind of shame that a woman feels, if she consents to an exchange of letters—shameful indeed, but not such a feeling of deadly sickness as comes with the humiliating view of an object of admiration degraded. Bad she may be; and she may be deceived, vilely treated, in either case. And what is a woman's pride but the staff and banner of her soul, beyond all gifts? He who wounds it cannot be forgiven—never!—he has killed the best of her. Aminta found herself sliding along into the sentiment, that the splendid idol of a girl's worship is, if she discover him in the lapse of years as an infinitesimally small one, responsible for the woman's possible reckless fit of giddiness.

And she could see her nonsense; she could not correct it. Lines of the letters under signature of Adolphus were phosphorescent about her: they would recur; and she charged their doing so on the discovered meanness of the girl's idol. Her wicked memory was caused by his having plunged her low.

Mrs. Pagnell performed the offices of attention to Mr. Weyburn in lieu of the countess, who seemed to find it a task to sit at the luncheon table with him, when Lady Ormont was absent. "Just peeped in," she said, as she entered the library, " to see if all was comfortable ; " and gossip ensued, not devoid of object. She extracted an astonishingly smooth description of Lady Charlotte. Weyburn was brightness in speaking of the much-misunderstood lady. "She's one of the *living* women of the world."

"You are sure you don't mean one of

the worldly women?" Mrs. Pagnell rejoined.

"She has to be known to be liked," he owned.

"And you were, one hears, among the favoured?"

"I can scarcely pretend to that, ma'am."

"You were recommended."

"Lady Charlotte is devoted to her brother."

Mrs. Pagnell's bosom heaved. "How strange Lord Ormont is! One would suppose, with his indignation at the country for its treatment of him, admirers would be welcome. Oh dear, no! that is not the way. On board the packet, on our voyage to Spain, my niece in her cabin, imploring mercy of Neptune, as they say, I heard of Lord Ormont among the passengers. I could hardly credit my ears. For I had been hearing of him from my niece ever since her return from a select establishment for the education of young ladies, not much more than a morning's drive out of London, though Dover was my residence. She had got a hero! It was Lord Ormont! Lord Ormont! all day: and when the behaviour of the country to him became notorious, Aminta—my niece the countess—she could hardly contain herself. A secret: —I promised her—it's not known to Lord Ormont himself:—a printed letter in a metropolitan paper, copied into the provincial papers, upholding him for one of the greatest of our patriot soldiers and the saviour of India, was the work of her hands. You would, I am sure, think it really well written. Meeting him on deck —the outline of the coast of Portugal for an introductory subject, our Peninsular battles and so forth—I spoke of her enthusiasm. The effect was, to cut off all communication between us. I had only to appear, Lord Ormont vanished. I said to myself, this is a character. However, the very mention of him to my niece, as one of the passengers on board—medicine, miraculous! She was up in half-an-hour, out pacing the deck before evening, hardly leaning on my arm, and the colour positively beginning to show on her cheeks again. He fled, of course. I had prepared her for his eccentricities. Next morning she was out by herself. In the afternoon Lord Ormont strode up to us—his military step—and most courteously requested the honour of an introduction. I had broken the ice at last; from that moment he was cordiality itself, until—I will not say, until he had called her his own—a few little misunderstandings!—not with his countess. You see, a resident aunt is translated mother-in-law by husbands; though I spare them pretty frequently; I go to friends, they travel. Here in London she must have a *dueña*.—The marriage at Madrid, at the

Embassy :—well, perhaps it was a step for us, for commoners, though we rank with the independent. Has her own little pin-money—an inheritance. Perhaps Lady Eglett gives the world her version. She may say, there was aiming at station. I reply, never was there a more whole-hearted love-match! Absolutely the girl's heart has been his from the period of her schooldays. Oh! a little affair—she was persecuted by a boy at a neighbouring school. Her mistress wrote me word—a very determined Romeo young gentleman indeed—quite alarmed about him. In the bud! I carried her off on the spot, and snapped it effectually. Warned he meant to be desperate, I kept her away from my house at Dover four months, place to place; and I did well. I heard on my return, that a youth, answering to the schoolmistress's description of him, had been calling several times, the first two months and longer.

You have me alluding to these little nonsensical nothings, because she seemed born to create violent attachments, even at that early day; and Lady Eglett—Lady Charlotte Eglett may hear; for there is no end to them, and impute them to her, when really!—can she be made responsible for eyes innocent of the mischief they appear destined to do? But I am disturbing you in your work."

"You are very good, ma'am," said the ghost of the determined young gentleman.

"A slight cold, have you?" Mrs. Pagnell asked solicitously.

"Dear me, no!" he gave answer with a cleared throat.

In charging him with more than he wanted to carry, she supplied him with particulars he had wanted to know; and now he asked himself what could be the gain of any amount of satisfied curiosity regarding a married Aminta. She slew my lord on board a packet-boat; she bears the arrows that slay. My lord married her where the first English chaplain was to be found; that is not wonderful either. British Embassy, Madrid! Weyburn believed the ceremony to have been performed there: at the same time, he could hear Lady Charlotte's voice repeating with her varied intonation Mrs. Pagnell's impressive utterances; and he could imagine how the somewhat silly duenna aunt, so penetrable in her transparent artifices, struck emphasis on the incredulity of people inclined to judge of the reported ceremony by Lord Ormont's behaviour to his captive.

How explain that strange matter? But can there be a gain in trying to sound it? Weyburn shuffled it away. Before the fit of passion seized him, he could turn his eager mind from anything which had not a perceptible point of gain, either for bodily strength or mental acquisition, or for money, too, now that the school was growing palpable as an infant in arms and agape for the breast. Thought of gain, and the bent to pursue it, is the shield of Athene over young men in the press of the seductions. He had to confess his having lost some bits of himself by reason of his meditations latterly; and that loss, if we let it continue a space, will show in cramp at the wrist, logs on the legs, a wheezy wind, for any fellow vowed to physical trials of strength and skill. It will show likewise in the brain beating broken wings—inability to shoot a thought up out of the body for half a minute. And, good Lord! how quickly the tight-strung fellow crumbles, when once the fragmentary disintegration has begun! Weyburn cried out on a heart that bounded off at prodigal gallops, and had to be nipped with reminders of the place of good leader he was for taking among the young. Hang superexcellence! but we know those moanings over the troubles of a married woman; we know their sources, know their goal, or else we are the fiction-puppet or the Bedlamite; and she is a married woman, married at the British Embassy, Madrid, if you please! after a few week's acquaintance with her husband, who doubtless wrote his name intelligibly in the registrar's book, but does not prove himself much the hero when he drives a pen, even for so little as the signing of his name! He signed his name, apparently not more than partly pledging himself to the bond. Lord Ormont's autobiographical scraps combined with Lady Charlotte's hints and Mrs. Pagnell's communications, to provoke the secretary's literary contempt of his behaviour to his wife. However, the former might be mended, and he resumed the task.

It had the restorative effect of touching him to see his old hero in action; whereby he was brought about to a proper modesty, so that he really craved no more than for the mistress of this house to breathe the liberal air of a public acknowledgment of her rightful position. Things constituted by their buoyancy to float are remarkable for lively bobbings when they are cast upon the waters; and such was the case with Weyburn, until the agitation produced by Mrs. Pagnell left him free to sail away in the society of the steadiest.

He decided that by not observing, not thinking, not feeling, about the circumstances of the household into which Fate had thrown him, he would best be able—probably it was the one way—to keep himself together; and his resolution being honest all round, he succeeded in it as long as he abstained from a very wakeful vigilance over simple eyesight. For if one is nervously on guard to not-see, the matter starts up winged, and enters us, and kindles the mind, and tingles through the blood; it has us as a foe. The art of blind vision requires not only practice, but an intimate knowledge of the arts of the traitor we carry within. Safest for him, after all, was to lay fast hold of the particularly unimportant person he was, both there and anywhere else. The Countess of Ormont's manner toward him was to be read as a standing index of the course he should follow; and he thanked her. He could not quite so sincerely thank her aunt. His ingratitude for the sickly dose she had administered to him sprang a doubt whether Lady Ormont now thanked her aunt on account of services performed at the British Embassy, Madrid.

Certain looks of those eyes recently, when in colloquy with my lord, removed the towering nobleman to a shadowed landscape.

Was it solely an effect of eyes commanding light, and having every shaft of the quiver of the rays at her disposal? Or was it a shot from a powerful individuality issuing out of bondage to some physical oppressor no longer master of the soul, in peril of the slipping away of the body? Her look on him was not hate: it was larger, more terribly divine. Those eyes had elsewhere once looked love: they had planted their object in a throbbing Eden. The man on whom they had looked shivered over the thought of it after years of blank division.

Rather than have those eyes to look on him their displacing unintentness, the man on whom they had once looked love would have chosen looks of wrath, the darts that kill—blest darts of the celestial Huntress, giving sweet sudden cessation of pain, in the one everlasting last flash of life with thought that the shot was hers. Oh for the ἀγανὰ βέλεα of the Merciful in splendour!

These were the outcries of the man

deciding simultaneously not to observe, not to think, not to feel, and husbanding calculations upon storage of gain for the future. Softness held the song below. It came of the fact that his enforced resolution, for the sake of sanity, drove his whole reflective mind backward upon his younger days, when an Evening and a Morning star in him greeted the bright Goddess Browny or sang adieu, and adored beyond all golden beams the underworld whither she had sunk, where she was hidden.

Meanwhile, the worthy dame who had dosed him was out in her carriage, busy paying visits to distinguished ladies of the great world, with the best of excuses for an early call, which was gossip to impart, such as the Countess of Ormont had not yet thought of mentioning; and two or three of them were rather amusedly interested to hear that Lord Ormont had engaged a handsome young secretary, "under the patronage of Lady Charlotte Eglett, devoted to sports of all kinds, immensely favoured by both." Gossip must often have been likened to the winged insect bearing pollen to the flowers; it fertilizes many a vacuous reverie. Those flowers of the upper garden are not, indeed, stationary and in need of the missionary buzzer, but if they have been in one place unmoved for one hour, they are open to take animation from their visitors. Aminta was pleasantly surprised next day by the receipt of a note from Mrs. Lawrence Finchley, begging to be invited to lunch if she came, as she had a purpose in the wish to meet my lord.

CHAPTER VIII.

MRS. LAWRENCE FINCHLEY.

My lord had one of his wilful likings for Isabella Lawrence Finchley, and he consented to the torture of an hour of Mrs. Nargett Pagnell in the middle of the day, just to taste the favourite he welcomed at home as he championed her abroad. The reasons were numerous and intimate why she pleased him. He liked the woman, enjoyed the cause for battle that she gave. Weyburn, on coming to the luncheon table, beheld a lady with the head of a comely boy, the manner, softened in delicate feminine, of a capital comrade. Her air of candour was her nature in her face; and it carried a guileless roguery, a placid daring, a supersensual naughtiness, a simplicity of repose amid the smoky reputation she created, that led one to think the vapour calumnious or the creature privileged. That young boy's look opened him at once; he had not to warm to her,—he flew. Ordinarily the sweetest ladies will make us pass through cold mist and cross a stile or two, or a broken bridge, before the formalities are cleared away to grant us rights of citizenship. She was like those frank lands where we have not to hand out a passport at the frontier and wait for dubious inspection of it.

She prevailed with cognizant men and with the frivolous. Women were capable of appreciating her, too; as Aminta did, despite some hinted qualifications addressed shyly to her husband. But these were the very matters exciting his particular esteem. He was of Lady Charlotte's mind, in her hot zeal against injustice done to the creatures she despised; and yet more than she applauded a woman who took up her idiot husband's challenge to defend her good name, and cleared it, right or wrong, and beat him down on his knees, and then started for her spell of the merry canter over turf: an example to the English of the punishment they get for their stupid Puritanic tyranny—sure to be followed by a national helter-skelter down-hill headlong. And Mrs. Lawrence was not one of the corrupt, he argued: she concealed what it was decent to conceal, without pouting hypocritical pretences; she had merely dispensed with idle legal formalities, in the prettiest curvetting airy wanton way, to divorce the man who tried to divorce her, and " whined to be forgiven when he found he couldn't. Adderwood was ready to marry her to-morrow, if the donkey husband would but go and bray his last.

Half-a-dozen others were heads off on the same course to that goal."

That was her champion's perusal of a lady candidly asserting her right to have breeched comrades, and paying for it in the advocacy which compromises. She was taken to be and she was used as a weapon wherewith to strike at our Pharisees. Women pushing out into the world for independence, bleed heavy payments all round.

The earl's double-edged defence of her was partly a vindication of another husband, who allowed his wife to call her friend; he was nevertheless assured of her not being corrupt, both by his personal knowledge of the lady, and his perception of her image in the bosom of his wife. She did no harm there, he knew well. Although he was not a man to put his trust in faces, as his young secretary inclined to do, Mrs. Lawrence's look of honest boy did count among the pleadings. And somewhat so might a government cruiser observe the intrusion of a white-sailed yacht in protected sea-waters, where licenced trawlers are at the haul.

Talk over the table coursed as fluently as might be, with Mrs. Pagnell for a boulder in the stream. Uninformed by malice, she led up to Lord Adderwood's name, and perhaps more designedly spoke of Mr. Morsfield, on whom her profound reading into the female heart of the class above her caused her to harp, as "a real Antinous," that the ladies might discuss him and Lord Ormont wax meditative.

Mrs. Lawrence pitied the patient gentleman, while asking him in her mind who was the author of the domestic burden he had to bear.

"It reminds me, I have à mission," she said. "There's a fencing match down at a hall in the West, near the barracks; private and select; Soldier and Civilian; I forget who challenged — Civilian, one judges; Soldiers are the peaceful party. They want you to act 'umpire,' as they call it, on the military side, my dear lord; and you will? —I have given my word you will bring Lady Ormont. You will?—and not let me be confounded! Yes, and we shall make a party. I see consent. Aminta will enjoy the switch of steel. I love to see fencing. It rouses all that is diabolical in me."

She sent a skimming look at the secretary sitting opposite.

"And I," said he, much freshened.

"You fence?"

"Handle the foils."

"If you must speak modestly! Are you in practice?"

"I spend an hour in Captain Chiallo's fencing rooms generally every evening before dinner. I heard there the first outlines of the match proposed. You are right; it was the civilian."

"Mr. Morsfield, as I suspected."

She smiled to herself, like one saying, Not badly managed, Mr. Morsfield!

"Italian school?" Lord Ormont inquired, with a screw of the eyelids.

"French, my lord."

"The only school for teaching."

"The simplest—has the most rational method. Italians are apt to be tricky. But they were masters once, and now and then they send out a fencer the French can't touch."

"How would you account for it?"

"If I had to account for it, I should say, hotter blood, cool nerve, quick brain."

"Hum. Where are we, then?"

"We don't shine with the small sword."

"We had men neatly pinked for their slashings in the Peninsula."

"We've had clever Irishmen."

"Hot enough blood! This man Morsfield—have you crossed the foils with him?"

"Goes at it like a Spaniard; though Spaniards in Paris have been found wary enough."

My lord hummed. "Fellow looks as if he would easily lose his head over steel."

"He can be dangerous."

The word struck on something, and rang.

Mrs. Lawrence had a further murmur within her lips. Her travelling eye met Aminta's and passed it.

"But not dangerous, surely, if the breast is padded?" said Mrs. Pagnell.

"Oh no, oh no; not in that case!" Mrs. Lawrence ran out her voluble assent, and her eyelids blinked; her fair boy's face was mischief at school under shadow of the master.

She said to Weyburn: "Are you one in

the list—to give our military a lesson? They want it."

His answer was unheard by Aminta. She gathered from Mrs. Lawrence's pleased sparkle that he had been invited to stand in the list; and the strange, the absurd spectacle of a young schoolmaster taking the heroic attitude for attack and defence wrestled behind her eyes with a suddenly vivid first-of-May cricketing-field, a scene of snowballs flying, the vision of a strenuous lighted figure scaling to noble young manhood. Isabella Lawrence's look at him spirited the bright past out of the wretched long-brown-coat shroud of the present, prompting her to grieve that some woman's hand had not smoothed a small tuft of hair, disorderly on his head a little above the left parting, because Isabella Lawrence Finchley could have no recollection of how it used to toss feathery-wild at his games.

My lord hummed again. " I suspect

we're going to get a drubbing. This fellow here has had his French *maître d'armes*. Show me your hand, sir."

Weyburn smiled, and extended his right hand, saying: "The wrist wants exercise."

"Ha! square thumb, flesh full at the nail's ends; you were a bowler at cricket."

"Now examine the palms, my lord; I judge by the lines of the palms," Mrs. Pagnell remarked.

He nodded to her and rose.

Coffee had not been served, she reminded him; it was coming in, so down he sat a yard from the table; outwardly equable, inwardly cursing coffee, though he refused to finish a meal without his cup.

"I think the palms do betray something," said Mrs. Lawrence; and Aminta said: "Everything betrays."

"No, my dear," Mrs. Pagnell corrected her; "the extremities betray, and we cannot read the centre. Is it not so, my lord?"

"It may be as you say, ma'am."

She was disappointed in her scheme to induce a general examination of palms, and especially his sphinx lordship's.

Weyburn controlled the tongue she so frequently tickled to an elvish gavotte, but the humour on his face touched Mrs. Lawrence's to a subdued good-fellow roguishness, and he felt himself invited to chat with her on the walk for a reposeful ten minutes in Aminta's drawing-room.

Mrs. Pagnell, "quite enjoying the company," as she told her niece, was dismayed to hear her niece tell her of a milliner's appointment, positive for three o'clock; and she had written it in her head "p.m., four o'clock," and she had mislaid or destroyed the milliner's note; and she still had designs upon his lordship's palms, things to read and hint around her off the lines. She departed.

Lord Ormont became genial; and there was no one present who did not marvel that he should continue to decree a state of circumstances more or less necessitating the infliction he groaned under. He was too lofty to be questioned, even by his favourites. Mrs. Lawrence conjured the ghost of Lady Charlotte for an answer: this being Lord Adderwood's idea. Weyburn let his thoughts go on fermenting. Pride froze a beginning stir in the bosom of Aminta.

Her lord could captivate a reluctant woman's bosom when he was genial. He melted her and made her call up her bitterest pride to perform its recent office. That might have failed; but it had support in a second letter received from the man accounted both by Mrs. Lawrence and by Mr. Weyburn 'dangerous'; and the thought of who it was that had precipitated her to "play little games" for the sole sake of rousing him through jealousy to a sense of righteous duty, armed her desperately against him. She could exult in having read the second letter right through on receipt of it, and in remembering certain phrases; and notably in a reflection shot across her bewildered brain by one of the dangerous man's queer mad sentences: *Be as iron as you like, I will strike you to heat;* and her thought: *Is there assurance of safety in a perpetual defence?*—all while she smiled on her genial lord, and signified agreement, with a smiting of wonderment at her heart, when he alluded to a panic shout of the country for defence, and said: "Much crying of that kind weakens the power to defend when the real attack comes." Was it true?

"But say what you propose?" she asked.

Lord Ormont proposed vigilance and

drill; a small degree of self-sacrifice on the part of the population, and a look-out head in the War Department. He proposed to have a nation of stout braced men laughing at the foreign bully or bandit, instead of being a pack of whimpering women; whom he likened to the randomly protestant geese of our country roadside, heads out a yard in a gabble of defence while they go backing.

So thereupon Aminta's notion of a resemblance in the mutual thought subsided; she relapsed on the cushioning sentiment that she was a woman. And—only a woman! he might exclaim, if it pleased him; though he would never be able to say she was one of the whimpering. She, too, had the choice to indulge in scorn of the superior man stone blind to proceedings intimately affecting him—if he cared! One might doubt it.

Mrs. Lawrence listened to him with a

mind more disengaged, and a flitting disapproval of Aminta's unsympathetic ear, or reluctance to stimulate the devout attention a bruised warrior should have in his tent. She did not press on him the post of umpire. He consented—at her request, he said—to visit the show; but refused any official position that would, it was clearly enough implied, bring his name in any capacity whatever before the country which had unpardonably maltreated him.

Feminine wits will be set working, when a point has been gained; and as Mrs. Lawrence could now say she had persuaded Lord Ormont to gratify her specially, she warmed to fancy she read him, and that she might have managed the wounded and angry giant. Her minor intelligence, caracoling unhampered by harassing emotions, rebuked Aminta's for not perceiving that to win him round to whatever a woman may desire, she must be with him, outstrip him even, along the line he chooses for himself; abuse the country, rail at the Government, ridicule the title of English Army, proscribe the name of India in his hearing. Little stings of jealousy are small insect bites, and do not pique a wounded giant hardly sensible of irritation under his huge, and as we assume for our purpose, justifiable wrath. We have to speculate which way does the giant incline to go? and turn him according to the indication.

Mrs. Lawrence was driven by her critic mood to think Aminta relied—erroneously, after woman's old fashion—on the might of superb dark eyes after having been captured. It seemed to her worse than a beautiful woman's vanity, a childishness. But her boy's head held boy's brains; and Lord Ormont's praise of the splendid creature's nerve when she had to smell powder in

Spain, and at bull-fights, and once at a wrecking of their carriage down a gully on the road over the Alpujarras, sent her away subdued, envious, happy to have kissed the cheek of the woman who could inspire it.

END OF VOL. I.

www.ingramcontent.com/pod-product-compliance
Lightning Source LLC
Chambersburg PA
CBHW031742230426
43669CB00007B/440